95°00' E · · · 95°15' E

0 miles 10
0 kilometers 14

Yigrong

19,226 ft
5,860 m

14,081 ft
4,292 m

Po Tsangpo

SZECHWAN TIBET ROAD

Po Tsangpo

Pelung

Support team roadhead

30°00' N

SZECHWAN TIBET ROAD

Rong Chu

Po Tsangpo

17,884 ft
5,451 m

17,159 ft
5,230 m

18,140 ft
5,529 m

30°00' N

The 1998
Kayak Descent and Foot Traverse
in the
TSANGPO GORGES
OF TIBET

Mendung

•Gompo Ne

21,647 ft
6,598 m

Gyala Pelri
23,461 ft 7,151 m

*Walker and Phillips foot route
for support and exit.*

Payi•   *Tsangpo*

Rainbow Falls
(mile 44)

"Panther Beach"

29°45' N

Accident
Site

Tsangpo

Pemakochung•

29°45' N

16,004 ft
4,878 m

16,109 ft
4,910 m

Gyala•

23,458 ft
7,150 m

*Namcha Barwa
(Namjagbarwa Feng)*
25,446 ft 7,756 m

15,640 ft
4,767 m

*Wetherbee and Castillo foot route
for support and videography.*

Tsangpo

18,465 ft
5,628 m

Put-in

Pei ◄

17,234 ft
5,253 m

29°30' N

--- Kayak route
••• Foot trail
→ Direction of river flow
— Unimproved road

Inset map

CHINA
Tibet   AREA
ENLARGED

PAKISTAN   *Tsangpo*

HIMALAYA
NEPAL
BHUTAN
Brahmaputra

Ganges

MYANMAR
(BURMA)   LAOS

INDIA

BANGLADESH

THAILAND

ARABIAN SEA

BAY
OF
BENGAL

0   500 mi
0   750 km

SRI
LANKA

95°00' E

COURTING
THE
DIAMOND
SOW

COURTING THE DIAMOND SOW

A WHITEWATER EXPEDITION ON TIBET'S FORBIDDEN RIVER

Wickliffe W. Walker

ADVENTURE PRESS

NATIONAL GEOGRAPHIC
WASHINGTON, D. C.

First Printing September, 2000
ISBN # 0-7922-7960-3

Printed in U.S.A.

Interior design by Suez Kehi Corrado
Illustrations by Anita Hinders

COURTING
THE
DIAMOND
SOW

IN THE FALL OF 1986, Doug Gordon and I paddled around the bend of a Mexican river to encounter one of the most dramatic sights in white-water sport. I wrote at the time:

The Santa Maria flows in a slick green curve between steep limestone walls. From the left, the tributary Gallinas River leaps off the cliffs, falling cleanly almost 300 feet into the Santa Maria. The afternoon sun forms rainbows, sometimes two or more, in the mist. Jade-green-moss clings to polished rock sidewalls. And a roar, deeper and steadier than thunder, pulses through the canyon.

As with so many truly beautiful things, there is more than a little danger to the Tamul Falls. Close to the plummeting tons of water, sheets of spray, driven horizontally by hurricane winds, hit like ocean waves. There is no route downstream.

The spell cast by the power and terrible beauty of fast-moving rivers can be irresistible. For almost four decades, in various combinations on several continents, a small group of us were privileged to participate in the emergence of a new and thrilling sport. We were honored to represent the United States as our fledgling white-water racing grew to World Cup and Olympic levels, and we eagerly expanded our river-running horizons from weekend excursions to expeditions around the globe.

That enchantment drew us to Tibet in the autumn of 1998, where the Tsangpo River hurtles through great Himalayan gorges considered a symbolic representation of the deity Dorje Phagmo—the Diamond Sow—at once crystalline beauty and brute.

This account of our journey is dedicated to the memory of Doug.

CONTENTS

Introduction

QUIT RIVER SPORT for good thirty years ago. My brother Tom and I had spent the summer of 1970 racing Whitewater Slalom on rivers throughout backwoods Europe, a perhaps quixotic quest toward the 1972 Olympic games in Munich. But I placed dismally in the fall races back in the United States. Enough, I decided. I was a freshman at Yale; I had plenty of other things to think about. Tom said nothing to dissuade me.

But it was perhaps cannily that he took me along to Farmington, Connecticut, for the first race of the spring season, "just to get away from the campus." There I ran into my brother's former canoe partner and classmate, Wick Walker. I can still remember the penetrating look that Wick gave me, as we stood beside the churning snow melt of the first spring race, and I told him I was quitting. Wick would be my rival for one of the precious three spots on the Olympic team; yet he took great trouble to convince me, in the most courteous and circumspect way possible, that it would be foolish not to try to make the team. I left the racecourse that afternoon to go build a new racing boat for the season. And it turned out there was room on the team for both of us.

There were several more ins and outs over the next twenty

years. But after racing doubles, with Lecky Haller, in the 1992 Olympics I finally and decisively retired from whitewater racing. Lecky found a new partner. Doug Gordon, who for years had trained with me in Connecticut, moved to Salt Lake City to pursue his Ph.D. in Chemistry. Those I had paddled with for years had drifted off. For exercise I took to running and biking and lifting weights—all rather desultorily.

But Doug had never been just a racer, and with his move to Salt Lake City he did not stop boating. Like Wick and Tom— and sometimes along with them—he had long been an expedition boater. When Doug called me in 1995 to be one of a three-man descent of a remote British Columbia river—"we'll hire a float plane to do the shuttle"—it was with some relief that I began goal-oriented training once more. That was the Homothko river: paddling, scouting, portaging, hauling our boats up and down cliffsides, ringing our bells to let the bears know we were there. The next year we ran the Dean, also in British Columbia.

When Wick and Tom proposed a trip to the Tsangpo gorges, and Doug, too, signed on, I was eager for this new challenge: two months in Tibet.

"Never again," I said to my wife by satellite phone, from a hand-hewn house in the remote village of Mendung, five days' hike out of the river gorge but still two days short of the nearest road, while the pigs grunted from the bottom level, and the householder, Peme Gompa, coming up the stairs, checked his legs for leeches. I was done with expeditions, finished, through. As for Tibet, I wished I had never seen it.

A year later, the leaves began to turn in New England. The

small yellow ones, in particular, made me think of October in the Himalaya. Other impressions surfaced: mountains in the sky, broad-faced yaks, the sour smell of wild Tibetan fruit, the magnified chaos of large volumes of falling water.

I NOW REALIZE THAT I DO WANT TO GO BACK TO TIBET. I even want to launch once more onto the Tsangpo. Why? Just to be there.

I doubt that I will really return. But, strangely, I appreciate that renewed desire. It connects today's self with the one that set forth with my friends in October of 1998. And it allows me to read Wick's narrative with a full mixture of regret, nostalgia, and indefinable pleasure.

— JAMIE McEWAN
AUGUST, 2000

PROLOGUE

W E HAD BEEN FOLLOWING the river as it gnawed its way through the Himalaya.... Every day the scene grew more savage; the mountains higher and steeper; the river more fast and furious.... As the river, rushing like a lost soul between the hot hell in the heart of the Himalaya and the cold hell on the wind-swept peaks which guard the gorge, grew more dynamic, as the scenery grew harsher, and the thunder of the water more minatory, the touch of Nature came marvellously to the rescue. Everywhere, by cliff and rock and scree, by torn scar and ragged rent, wherever vegetation could get and keep a grip, trees grew; and so, from the grinding boulders in the river-bed to the grating glaciers above, the gorge was filled with forest to the very brim. Ten thousand feet of forest coloured those cold grey rocks of tortured gneiss; and when the summer rain weeps softly over the scene of riot a million trees will flame into flower and strew their beauty over the ruin.[1]

So legendary British explorer and plant hunter Frank Kingdon Ward described Tibet's great gorge of the Tsangpo in the winter of 1924. When Tom McEwan and I slowly worked our way along the riverbank of jumbled, moss-slicked boulders at a place named Chu Belap, our 50-year-old legs were aching from 4,000 feet of constant descent and our hands were ripped from checking our muddy slide down the mountain by gripping bamboo creepers like climbing ropes. But we had arrived at Kingdon Ward's ultimate point, as deep in the inner gorge as he or any other Western explorer had ever penetrated. It was November 3, 1997; our journey through many previous gorges had been a long one, and an even greater journey lay ahead.

TOM MCEWAN AND I HAVE BEEN CLOSE, if unlikely, friends since seventh grade. He was the consummate athlete, a champion wrestler and a football star. He was also impervious (or at least oblivious) to cold, exhaustion, or pain, with an otherworldly bent that would lead him to the 19th-century German philosophers while at Yale, and later to born-again Christianity. I was smaller, less wiry, and totally consumed with the more solitary outdoor challenges. I immersed myself in the writings of W. Douglas Burdon, Kermit Roosevelt, Jim Corbett, Eric Shipton, and H.W. Tilman. My sports would be means of transportation, not ends in themselves, and my intellectual flights would not soar much beyond the practical, if sometimes daunting, requirements of travel in hard, wild places. Tom's passion was that of a physicist, mine that of an engineer.

Our chance discovery, over a lunch table at the Landon School in a Maryland suburb, of a mutual fascination with canoeing occurred at a fortuitous time and place. In the late 1950s and early 1960s, Washington, D.C., was—as it is now—a center for the emerging sport of white-water canoeing and kayaking. Mentored by the dedicated cadre of adults who founded Washington's Canoe Cruisers Association, we plunged into the Potomac River on a course that was to shape our lives. Running local white-water streams in an aluminum canoe soon led to testing ourselves in races along the East Coast, and our success encouraged us toward the specialized, enclosed fiber-glass boats just then being developed.

Departure to different colleges, followed by a roving military career for me, ended our partnership in the two-man canoe. For both of us, though, the high school infatuation evolved into a lifetime romance with rivers, and like a braided stream our paths were to separate and rejoin time and again. I was assigned to the Washington, D.C., area in the early seventies—after college, the Olympics, and Vietnam—and the partnership resumed. Tom now paddled a one-man kayak; I used a solo slalom canoe (or C-1 in white-water terminology); and we ranged up and down the East Coast searching out difficult new runs. Some runs, such as the Meadow River of West Virginia, had recently been pioneered by others; some, including the Linville Gorge of North Carolina, we did not complete; and others, like the Great Falls of the Potomac outside Washington D.C., were first descents. From each we learned, grew in both confidence in ourselves and respect for the rivers, and sought new challenges.

Swayed by my long fascination with the literature of climbing, our ambitions turned to international white-water expeditions, then almost unknown. We began detailed planning for a first foray into the Himalaya of Bhutan, but that dream was not to be realized until my return from a military tour in Germany (time well invested running rivers with Europe's exploration paddling club, the Alpiner Kajak Club of Munich). My return to the States in the early 1980s allowed Tom and me to reunite, carry out the Bhutan experiment, and then continue with a series of expeditions in Mexico and Canada that were more economical and closer to home.

We did not paddle in a vacuum, of course. Our sport was growing as we were: Racers reached new levels we had never dreamed of; others, including my fellows in the Alpiner Kajak Club, were pursuing similar dreams of international expeditions; commercial river-running by raft and kayak grew geometrically not only in West Virginia but also in Chile, Costa Rica, and Nepal. Within our own small circle, Tom and I were accompanied by a short but growing list of talented paddlers with similar interests, foremost of whom was Tom's younger brother Jamie.

In 1988 an interviewer from *Canoe* magazine asked what my future ambition was, and I replied it was to "run the riverine equivalent of Mount Everest." I deliberately did not specify where that river might be, even though Tom and I had been planning for several years to make an expedition to the Tsangpo. No one argues that Everest is the most difficult achievement in mountaineering, but at least it is demonstrably the highest. For white-water rivers there is not even that modicum of an objective standard; "longest," "steepest," and "greatest volume" are irrelevant, and even the difficulty ratings of individual rapids are part of a subjective scale that evolves dramatically each decade. Every paddler is free to choose his own "Everest River."

Now and then someone claims that a particular river gorge is "the deepest canyon on Earth," but this, too, is a nearly meaningless designation because there is no standard by which to measure such a statistic. How steep must canyon walls be to qualify? How does one compare the gargantuan, vegetated slopes rising more than 17,000 feet from the Tsangpo to the summits of Namcha Barwa and Gyala Pelri, across a gulf of 15 miles, to the barren, nearly vertical walls enclosing Peru's Colca Canyon?

As paddlers, we tried to appreciate the grandeur and challenge of each river and canyon, at least in our worthier moments ignoring statistics. Tom and I preferred to regard our secret goal not as the most difficult or deepest gorge on Earth; instead, it was the "greatest" gorge on the planet, for in every aspect the gorges of the Tsangpo were undeniably world-class in scale, white-water difficulty, ecology, geology, culture, and religion.

In hindsight, it is doubtful that our (or any paddlers') skills and experience in the 1980s were up to attempting the Tsangpo run. For better or worse, we were not to be tested, because the political obstacles to expeditions in Tibet, and particularly in Tibet's most sensitive military region, were at that time insurmountable. In addition to China's overall sensitivity to Westerners traveling in Tibet for political and religious reasons, a long-standing border dispute with India was centered exactly at the expedition area. This dispute had flared into open warfare before and still featured skirmishes downplayed by both sides. Observers were not welcome—unless they brought their checkbooks.

With a keen capitalist appreciation for supply and demand, China had instituted a policy of exacting huge permit fees to ascend the long-forbidden, unclimbed mountains under their control. For Namcha Barwa, enclosed by the horseshoe bend of the Tsangpo and then the highest yet-unsummited peak in the Himalaya, the price tag was one million dollars. China was also beginning to suspect that unrun rivers might have equal value in Western eyes.

As a result, the proposal we submitted in 1983 for a modest, lightweight expedition without involvement of television or other heavyweight sponsors received short shrift at the Chinese Embassy in Washington, D.C. Resigned, we turned our efforts toward more promising directions.

I retired from serious white-water pursuits in 1990, not having seen the Tsangpo nor expecting to get the chance. For 30 years I had responded to the question of how long I intended to paddle with a glib response—"as long as I'm having fun"—and for 30 years that issue required no further thought; paddling was, had been, and would be my way of life. But accumulating injuries had made maintaining my skills increasingly more time-consuming and painful, and, although experience and long habit still got me down difficult rivers relatively unscathed, a concern now settled in the back of my mind about my stamina and ability to react to long, difficult swims or other emergency demands. Suddenly, shockingly, as I drifted in an eddy near the left shore of Charlie's Choice rapid on Maryland's upper Youghiogheny River, for perhaps the hundredth time since I first ran the river in 1965, it dawned that this favorite, roller-coaster was, in fact, no longer fun. With this surprising realization, I found it remarkably easy to drop out of the sport that had literally consumed my adult life. Work and other interests, long put off, consumed me.

Conversely, through the 1990s Tom paddled more than ever. The kayak teaching program he had run for years as part of his family's summer day camp spun off into an independent, year-round kayaking school for youth and adults. Tom led trips annually to Mexico, Canada, and the American West, and he noted with pleasure that he was still growing with the sport even though the hot young paddlers, including his teenage son Andrew, now surpassed his own skills and stamina. He entered his 50s considering his paddling stronger than ever before and regularly running rivers we would not have attempted in our "prime."

Things would have continued, our lives moving in other directions and the Tsangpo out of mind, were it not for pioneering efforts by others equally fascinated by the unapproachable gorge and the instigation of two other friends of mine, Harry and Doris Wetherbee, a foreign service couple I came to know in Pakistan. Insatiable travelers fascinated with Central and South Asia, the Wetherbees were experienced campers with a variety of outdoor skills, but neither accomplished paddlers nor mountaineers. Unlike Tom and me, they never had any ambition to run the river themselves. They were completely undaunted by the seemingly insurmountable diplomatic, fund-raising, and organizational problems that would need to be overcome before even reaching the river; or at least they were undaunted by the prospect of encouraging Tom and me to take it on.

Intrigued and caught up in the romance of the region when I first mentioned it to him in the winter of 1996-97, Harry banged out from the small computer room in his McLean, Virginia, home for more information. A copy of Kingdon Ward's *The Riddle of the Tsangpo Gorges* appeared through interlibrary loan from a rare book library. A map published by F.M. Bailey in 1914 was found and copied from a cooperative collector.[2] Soon maps and flags and the scanned images of previous explorers festooned the walls, and file folders grew on topics from potential sponsors to daily caloric requirements for mountaineers.

From the Internet, Harry developed a picture of the current political climate—encouragingly different from what we had found ten years previously. The Chinese still disputed the nearby border with India, but military tensions were reduced and the two countries had concluded a cease-fire in the early nineties. At about the same time, not entirely coincidentally, a team of Japanese climbers had finally negotiated a permit to climb Nanga Parbat with a joint Japanese/Chinese team. They were granted access to the area for three climbing seasons, and in 1992 they summited.

Americans were setting precedents as well. Richard Fisher, a tour promoter from Tucson, Arizona, organized several treks into the Tsangpo gorges between 1993 and 1994. On one of these, Jill Bielawski, Ken Storm, Ian Baker, and Eric Manthey became the first known Westerners to follow Kingdon Ward's route through the upper canyon since 1924. Storm and Baker were to return for various other noteworthy explorations throughout the decade. Also in 1993 veteran Everest climber David Breashears and photographer Gordon Wiltsie were in the canyon on assignment for NATIONAL GEOGRAPHIC magazine.[3]

White-water attempts had also been launched. The first attempts to raft the upper Yangtze, also in Tibet, came in 1988 by rival Chinese and American groups. And in 1993 two Japanese kayakers launched at the midpoint of the Tsangpo gorges; both swam in the first rapid and, sadly, Yoshitaka Takei was lost.

That same year, two of the groups organized by Richard Fisher attempted to raft the river just above the gorge but quickly concluded it was unfeasible. Two brothers, Gil and Troy Gillenwater, from one of these attempts would, like Baker and Storm, return for further expeditions on foot. Some of the political barriers to the Tsangpo might now be negotiated, but any whitewater descent was going to be extraordinarily difficult. And we were not alone in our ambition.

Harry's internet searches ultimately uncovered an American travel and expedition outfitter living and working from southern China; he had personal experience with the area and the arcane process of obtaining Chinese permits. As cautiously as any couple beginning an Internet romance, we and Jon Meisler in Chengdu began to sound each other out by e-mail across the Pacific. John already knew the climbing community, but, for him, the new world of white water was unknown territory when we contacted him. Moreover, we were not eager to see our still very tentative plans rumored around the paddling community or revealed yet to Chinese government officials. For his part, Jon was running a business in a world where there are many people with grand ideas; few, however, have the will, skill, or funding to carry out those ideas.

With the addition of Jon's considerable resources, several pieces of the puzzle now seemed to be fitting together. Nevertheless, both Tom and I knew that an attempt on the Tsangpo would be at an order of magnitude greater than anything we had tried before, and there were still huge unknowns. Only a full-scale expedition attempt, if not more than one, would determine whether a run down the river was possible, but planning such an effort without personal and firsthand experience of the area would likely lead to failure. The Internet can only take you so far.

BY THE SPRING OF 1997, TOM AND JAMIE MCEWAN, Harry and Doris Wetherbee, and I had committed ourselves to investing a year of hard work to accomplish an on-the-ground feasibility study. This we funded ourselves, maintaining the privacy of our plans and making easier the option of dropping the idea if we chose. In practical terms, approaching potential sponsors would be much more productive if we demonstrated this level of commitment and returned from Tibet with confidence that the expedition was a reasonable undertaking.

Jamie was disinclined to separate himself from his family for long trips two years in a row, so in September 1997, Tom, Harry, Doris, and I departed for Tibet on a monthlong "trekking tour." Meeting Jon Meisler in Chengdu, we proceeded through Lhasa to the region of the gorge, then down a foot trail to the midpoint of the river's gigantic, 140-mile horseshoe bend. There we divided forces: Harry and Doris proceeded downstream several miles with one group of local guides and porters, while Tom, Jon, and I followed Kingdon Ward's footsteps upstream, guided by local Monpa hunters, to get a glimpse of the most inaccessible inner gorge.

This was a "snapshot" view, a sample of the difficulties to be encountered, rather than an attempt to scout the entire river to determine whether each rapid could be run or portaged. That would be the task of the next, longer and better-equipped, expedition—if, in fact, there was one.

By the time that we arrived back in Lhasa in early November, we had accomplished several critical objectives while working with Jon Meisler and had built mutual respect. trust, and teamwork. We had: obtained access to the area from the Chinese and Tibetan authorities (their attitude might have been different toward a larger expedition with boats); obtained help, guides, and porters from the two most important villages on the route; experienced the weather and terrain during the season we projected would be the most promising for an expedition; and had field-tested communications between separate groups in the gorge, proving that our satellite telephones could "see" the satellites despite the mountain walls, and that they could hold up to the extraordinary weather conditions. Finally, we had seen and photographed between 10 and 15 percent of the critical river mileage—not as much as we had hoped, but enough to make some informed judgments.

None of those test cases went perfectly, and almost as many new problems were revealed as were overcome. Yet, we had gathered sufficient hope for a successful run. Upon our return to the United States we resolved to attempt a full-scale expedition to descend the Tsangpo gorges, using white-water boats as the primary tool. Through the Christmas period and into January we fleshed out a detailed plan for a 54-day expedition beginning in late September 1998.

I WAS TO BE THE OVERALL EXPEDITION LEADER, out front in the quest for permits and sponsorship, coordinating organizational details; in the field, I would direct from land the activities of both river and support teams. Tom would lead the core element, the four-man team who would descend the river by boat and on foot from the last road access before the great horseshoe bend. Ideally, the boat team would traverse 140 miles of river to a take-out point at the foot of a relatively easy pass leading across the neck of the bend and back to their starting place. They would carry supplies and equipment in their boats and travel independently for days at a stretch, while two support crews (each having two Americans and a Sherpa), with local porters, leapfrogged ahead to resupply them at intervals and assist with rescue and evacuation if necessary. The two Sherpas, from that tribal group living in the vicinity of Mount Everest who have been the backbone of Himalayan climbing for almost a century, spoke English and Tibetan, were experienced in the conduct of expeditions, and would be our bridge to the local tribesmen.

The spring and summer of 1998 were consumed by planning and preparation. Tom concentrated on the detailed boating plan, projecting times and locations for prearranged resupply points, working out with the other boaters the training required for the task ahead, and, of course, selecting the other paddlers. His brother Jamie was included from the earliest stages, and Doug Gordon, Jamie's best friend, joined early and enthusiastically. Doug had accompanied Tom and me on earlier expeditions. The remaining slot saw more turmoil, as two other experienced friends considered our invitation and then declined because of conflicting commitments to family, work, and other expeditions. By August, however, Roger Zbel—a veteran racer, river-runner, and rafting company operator long known to Tom and me—completed the river team. An old military friend of mine, former Green Beret medic Dave Phillips, volunteered to round out the support element.

Harry and Doris focused on logistic details, such as food, communications, and air transport for the team. Together with Doug they sought out manufacturers to donate essential equipment. Jamie assembled climbing equipment, prepared a book proposal, and coordinated with me about photographic coverage.

Obtaining permits was largely in the hands of Jon Meisler, while I applied for grants that would help pay for the permits, travel services, food, and communications—all items that could not be covered by advertising monies from equipment manufacturers. This was a roller-coaster ride. Early successes (and prestige) came in the form of a Malden Mills Polartec Challenge Grant, plus smaller grants from several individuals and the Henry Foundation for Botanical Research. Following long tradition, the Explorers Club in New York awarded the expedition one of its historic flags to carry, and the American Canoe Association endorsed the project and agreed to manage the funds. This was all succeeded by months of detailed and encouraging review by the Rolex Corporation in Geneva for one of their Awards for Enterprise. Then in June, having made it into the final group of 64 projects under final consideration, we were not selected. If we still intended to arrive in Tibet that autumn, by July the Chinese would require a large down payment and firm commitment to pay in advance for permits, transport, and other services.

We were seriously considering a year-long delay when the National Geographic Society's Expeditions Council approved our application for a grant in July. We were finally financially secure, although with little to spare. With the financing came a ninth team member: The Society wished to send videographer Paulo Castillo along with the support team to film as much as he could. Also in July the Chinese confirmed that they had approved permits for a combined "trekking and boating tour."

The reality began to sink in that we were actually on our way, that this was more than a massive paperwork exercise.

Throughout the winter, spring, and early summer we performed a kind of balancing act. A certain amount of self-promotion was required to impress potential sponsors and other supporters, but we didn't want to get involved in a competition with the several white-water groups now seriously interested in the Tsangpo. Although most of them were as circumspect about their plans as we were, it appeared that two Western groups, one primarily rafters and the other expedition kayakers, had serious plans but were not yet fully prepared; both were scouting in 1998, much as we had in the fall of 1997. As far as we knew, only a Chinese team was "in the field," and their intentions were completely unknown.

UNLIKE THE LARGELY MEANINGLESS ATTENTION paid to the Everest of Rivers or the deepest canyon in the world, there can be a certain amount of justified pride in accomplishing any first descent. The feat would be similar to a first ascent in climbing, and to achieve it on the great Tsangpo was our acknowledged goal.

The skills demanded of, and dangers presented to, each paddler in a rapid are no less for the thousandth run than for the first. Nevertheless, the exploration of any white-water river for the first time is, in fact, enormously more difficult than subsequent runs. The judgment and confidence required to analyze a route and then run a rapid that has never been tried before is qualitatively different. Seeing what the water does to another boater or knowing that a rapid has been run successfully on another occasion gives a measure of security and reduces the inherent stress.

Other factors complicate as well. First descents are often, perhaps usually, as much logistics and hiking exercises as they are white-water runs. Until routes of access and egress are known, the effects of different water levels are understood, and the difficulties to be found around each corner are predictable, enormous amounts of time and energy are devoted to these factors, which are taken for granted on well-established routes. In the interest of simply getting downstream, first-attempt teams frequently carry their boats around rapids later "worked out" and routinely run by subsequent groups with fewer other concerns. Consequently, first descents are rarely elegant processions downstream from start to finish, and it is not unusual for a first descent requiring multiple days to evolve into a routine run of a single day.

Just as many expert skiers eschew mountain touring, with its avalanche and crevasse hazards and its unpredictable snow conditions, to practice their craft on groomed slopes, many of the best white-water paddlers prefer the established runs, including man-made racecourses. Even among explorers, the judgment is subjective and personal about how much of a river must be run, and in what style, to fit the concept of a first descent. If rapids are carried around, what percentage? If run, does a "sneak route" along the shoreline count? And if explored during extremely low water, or in flood, what is the relationship to a normal descent? Like the white water itself, the term "first descent" eludes easy grasp.

Despite the difficulties and the ambiguity about definitions, the privilege of practicing our discipline in that great gorge was a prize beyond measure for us. We now had the means and the will to make the attempt, along with the full knowledge that there was an enormous distance between the suburbs of Washington, D.C., and our projected take-out point at Medog, Tibet.

CHAPTER 1

CROSSING TO TIBET

*We are ready to enter the mysterious canyon, and start with
some anxiety. The old mountaineers tell us that it cannot
be run...but all are eager for the trial, and off we go.*

—MAJOR JOHN WESLEY POWELL,
on the first descent of the Grand Canyon. 1869

ROGRESS IS NOT ALWAYS KIND. The village of
Kodari, on the border between Nepal and Tibet,
contrasts starkly with the serene, unearthly
beauty of the surrounding Himalaya.
Squalid, impermanent buildings of fieldstone and timber flank
muddy, pitted streets too narrow for two-way truck traffic.
Ravens and gray-headed crows contest with semiwild dogs
and pigs for the right to pick through trash piles of offal and
pastel plastic bags at either end of the village. Dense blends of
diesel fumes, smoke from fires of damp wood or yak dung, and
temple offerings of burnt juniper hang in layers between
valley walls.

One day in late September 1998, an avalanche of sheep,

goats, and children poured down a gully and into the main street, swirling and eddying around halted trucks, tourist buses, and our expedition team and piles of gear. Bright sun from a cloudless sky heated the crowded street by the Nepalese border station. This was the "October window," the precious few weeks of fair weather sometimes granted the Himalaya between summer's monsoon clouds from India and winter's winds from the steppes of Asia. Our party of nine Americans and two Sherpas sweated` and strained impatiently to push on to the high, cool Tibetan plateau.

Vehicles do not proceed beyond this point. Pedestrians clear the Nepalese immigration post, walk across the bridge that represents the formal border, and climb into Tibetan vehicles on the other side. Suddenly, in response to some signal invisible to us, our mountain of gear rose above the deluge of sheep and goats; it was placed on the backs of a crowd of local men eager for porter fees and then carried across the bridged ravine into Tibet. Four white-water boats, sheathed in black nylon bags to protect them from the rigors of travel by air and truck halfway around the globe, followed bundles of paddles, held together with duct tape, and 19 olive drab, oversize GI duffel bags containing three-quarters of a ton of freeze-dried food and camp gear. Still not cleared to proceed by Nepalese officialdom, we watched anxiously as our possessions disappeared into a very foreign country, into a remote land where so many mysteries, both physical and magical, remained at the close of the millennium, despite centuries of questing by pilgrims, explorers, scientists, and spies.

Neither impatience nor jet lag inhibited Doug Gordon's eager curiosity as he ranged up and down the short street, drinking in the exotic smells and sounds and sights. With his compact frame clad in blue shorts, polo shirt, and sandals, the black cord securing his dark glasses trailing down his neck like a skinny pony tail, and already a heavy shadow of emerging black beard on his cheeks, he looked like many another backpacker on the "Kathmandu Trail." His two personae, the highly respected scientist recently returned from an international conference in France, and the 22 year veteran of international competition and expedition kayaking, were both hidden for the moment, although both lay not far beneath the surface. At a small store front, he carefully spent all his remaining Nepalese rupees, filling his pockets with fruit for the long barren drive ahead and enjoying both the pantomime bargaining and the practicality of the exchange.

In the rear seat of one Toyota Land Cruiser, Tom McEwan sat reading, aloof equally from the chaos swirling around the vehicle and the mountain grandeur above. Like a deacon of some severe Scottish sect contemplating the human frailties of the congregation, he would glance occasionally at the ton of equipment, our crowd of vehicle drivers, guides, cooks, and porters, and the two Sherpas down from Namche Bazar on Everest. His *sotto voce* comment trailed off almost plaintively: "Who ARE all these people...?" His real question rang unspoken but clear. What have all these days of commercial travel, these mountains of equipment and supplies, and these crowds of support people and hangers-on to do with something as clean, clear, and simple as paddling an eggshell kayak down glacial water through a pristine canyon?

IN 1971, TOM AND HIS BROTHER JAMIE dreamed of places on the

1972 Olympic Team, a dream shared by the entire world of white-water sport, because that was the first year the young sport had been included in the most prestigious of all sporting events. But simply making the team would not suffice for Tom, nor even medaling. He must do it his own, clean, unencumbered way. Eschewing coaches, gyms, and organized competition, the brothers retreated into the winter hills of West Virginia, living in the back of their van, alternating solo runs down the icy rivers while the other drove to the take-out spot. Somehow, only emerging from this isolation to sweep the team trials and challenge the world would fit Tom's synthesis of hardheaded Scot family tradition and a Nietzschean outlook he had acquired at Yale.

In the end, this *gestalt* was never tested in the Olympic arena. A severe knee injury ended the dream for Tom, who spent the rest of the winter living from his kayak in the Okefenokee Swamp. For Jamie, the dream led to a formal training camp in California and the bronze medal in Munich. Now at 52, Tom's spare frame, lean face, and receding hairline seemed to indicate that maybe even body fat and hair, like the Ivy League degree he spurned so many years ago, were superfluous to the life of pure simplicity.

TOM'S WITHDRAWAL INTO HIS BOOK STOPPED SHORT of vocal objection. Like his Scots deacon alter ego, he admits the existence, even necessity, of many things he would prefer to avoid. Jointly, he and I had arrived at the present plan, concluding reluctantly that travel into terrain so vast and so remote would be foolhardy without external support and resupply. In any case we would not be allowed free rein to wander near the contested border region between India and China unencumbered by official guides and retinue. Our partnership in river trips reached back more than 35 years—to weekend canoe trips on the Potomac River before either of us could drive—and he seemed content to leave to me the myriad unsavory details of visas, equipment permits, sherpa hiring, sponsor solicitation, and the like. Tom would glance up periodically, perhaps because he knew my penchant for military-style planning and wanted to be sure I had not slipped in an extra platoon or two.

For my part, my co-leader's mental absence was expected. As we approached the village—in seven or eight days, more than four hundred miles to the east—where the four white-water paddlers would launch downriver, Tom would emerge rested and focused totally on his unique task: He would mold himself and three other enormously talented and experienced athletes into a team capable of kayaking through the greatest canyon on Earth, carved by the pounding cascades of one of Asia's major rivers through the little-explored eastern corner of the Himalayan Range.

Nepalese bureaucracy eventually gave forth papers, and we walked eagerly after our equipment, over the bridge crossing to Tibet.

CHAPTER 2

LONG
HARD
ROAD

There are no larger fields than these,
no worthier games than may here be played.

— HENRY DAVID THOREAU

 OLD RED LINES march resolutely across the map of Tibet, connecting ebony dots that proclaim major cities and administrative capitals. On this barren high plateau, however, these lines do not represent existing, rapid lines of transportation and communication; instead they symbolize the ambitions of Chinese engineers and social planners. These ambitions are being played out, rock by hand-carried rock, by hundreds of work gangs, who live at their work sites in nomad villages of plastic-sheathed huts and wage an almost stalemated trench warfare with the forces of flood and landslide.

We worked our way from Kodari up onto the Tibetan Plateau, around Everest and eastward in three Land Cruisers and one of China's ubiquitous blue Dong Feng (Eastern Wind) cargo trucks. Progress seemed unbelievably slow. Hours of waiting in long queues of lumber trucks and military convoys at blasting sites were only relieved by kidney-banging cross-country detours. Rare intervals of narrow, undisturbed gravel road consumed all but the lead vehicle in clouds of choking dust.

NEAR THE END OF SEPTEMBER, nights on the plateau already hinted at winter. Morning activity in our roadside camp was unenthusiastic until shadows of the eastern hills shortened and sunlight began to engulf the area. Only emergency traffic attempts the roads at night, but with daylight came the first rumbles and dust of cargo trucks. Soon after came the throaty roar of a kerosene stove from within the bulky gray canvas cook tent belonging to Ang Kami Sherpa and Pemba Sherpa. After various intervals, determined by individual estimates of how long it would take for the Sherpas' teapot to boil water, came the unzipping of sleeping bags and tents and the banging of truck doors as drivers emerged. A pile of driftwood and other flammable scraps ignited with a *whump* and a cloud of greasy smoke from massive kerosene encouragement.

Before the anticipated shafts of sunlight arrived, Roger Zbel had a nearby hilltop picked out as a hiking objective, a couple thousand feet above the camp. He was encouraging others to finish their oatmeal and muesli, coffee and hot chocolate, and "get moving." On his first trip to Asia (his previous international paddling had been in South America) and new to expedition paddling with this group, Roger was to some extent an outsider. His ready smile, ragged blond beard, and hint of middle-age complacence in face and waistline disguised a depth of physical and mental stamina that would emerge as the journey unfolded.

Because the cargo truck laden with expedition gear and camp equipment traveled more slowly than the three Land Cruisers carrying passengers, there was ample time for this morning workout while camp was struck, the truck loaded and dispatched in advance. Roger's eager pace up the braids of dusty goat trails ascending the hillside was easily matched by Pemba Sherpa, a shy 18-year-old finding this trip vastly different from his previous two expeditions on Everest. Tom McEwan and Doug Gordon set their own pace, bright rain jackets tied by the sleeves around their waists as they warmed to the climb. Behind, Jamie alternated bursts of speed with halts to take photos, while I pretended to admire the view as I caught my breath, keenly aware of almost 12,000 feet of elevation.

An hour later, with legs stretched and a certain amount of stress worked off, the group layered their air mattresses across the backseats of the Land Cruisers and settled in for another wracking day. The slow and confining drive, on the heels of days in the air and jet lag, was hardest on the expedition's four white-water paddlers: Tom, Jamie, Doug, and Roger. Partly this was the reaction of veteran athletes. Years of intensive training will program the body and mind beyond the point of just tolerating high levels of stress and activity to actually needing them. More powerful even than the metabolic changes—appetites, sleep patterns, and pulse rates associated with the daily "fix" of activity—are the mental imperatives. A day without the habitual workout provokes anxiety, for some an almost Calvinistic sense of guilt. Many elite racers, Jamie very much included, are prone to a sort of hypochondria where the slightest wrong thing, such as a minor injury, a missed meal, or a change of routine, can assume disastrous proportions. The most finely honed razor can be also the most brittle.

The four were all experienced in this sort (if not this degree) of international expedition travel, and they were mature enough to understand and, to some extent, head off these reactions. Inescapable, however, was the fact that their descent through the Tsangpo gorges by white-water canoe and kayak would be the heart and soul of the expedition, and it would present, by far, the greatest physical demand and danger. Success would depend on many factors, but one thing was certain: It would be impossible without every bit of skill, stamina, and focus the group possessed, and nothing could be allowed to dull their cutting edge.

Caravanning across the Roof of the World was a little easier for the expedition's "Swiss Army knives"—the support crew and myself. We had trained for months for the demanding trek that would be required of us, but our accustomed levels of physical activity were more "normal" and the anxiety and tension proportionally less from our secondary roles. Also, each individual of the support element had been selected because of long experience living and traveling throughout the developing world.

Paulo Castillo, the videographer attached to the expedition by National Geographic Television, had just returned from guiding a rafting trip on China's upper Yangtze River. Harry and Doris Wetherbee had lived years overseas in foreign service assignments that included the former Soviet Union, Ethiopia, Pakistan, and India. This was their third long trip into remote areas of China. Team medic Dave Phillips's career in developing world medical programs began in Green Beret camps in Vietnam's Montagnard villages and led through five continents in more than 30 years.

FIVE DAYS AND ALMOST 500 DUSTY, AXLE-POUNDING MILES of Tibetan "highway" to the east of Kodari lay the expedition's destination. By every measure, physical and metaphysical, the land was larger than life, an unspoiled place of romance and challenge. It was difficult to believe that such a place remained unexplored at the end of the 20th century.

In the vicinity of Tibet's sacred Mount Kailas, two of Asia's legendary rivers rise near the midpoint of the Himalayan massif. Flowing in opposite directions north of and parallel to the mountains, they drain the Roof of the World and, in the words of Swedish explorer Sven Hedin, "like a crab's claws, encircle the Himalayas." [1]

The Indus flows north and west beyond Kashmir. a troubled land of legendary beauty. At the western anchor of the mountain range, Nanga Parbat (Naked Mountain), the Indus finally breaks free of the plateau, thunders through the Rhondu gorges of Pakistan, and begins its long descent to the Indian Ocean beyond Karachi.

The Tsangpo flows south and east across the breadth of the Tibetan Plateau. Looping around the eastern anchor of the Himalaya, Namcha Barwa, the Tsangpo plunges off the heights of the plateau, dropping more than 9,000 feet to the plains of Assam, India, where it emerges renamed the Brahmaputra. The massive gorges, where the great river plummets through dramatic zigzag clefts in the heart of the mountains, contain some of the most formidable white water imaginable. The sporting challenge of the river is but one thread in a richer tapestry, however.

In Buddhist mythology the fantastic landscape of this Pemako (Land of Flowers) is the physical representation of the body of the recumbent goddess Dorje Phagmo (the Diamond Sow), one of several havens or sanctuaries hidden on the borders of Tibet and only accessible by the enlightened. From this legend sprang the novel about a place that has entered the English language as a symbol of paradise on Earth: Shangri-La.

For the last two centuries, the gorges have been as much a grail for Western explorers as for Eastern pilgrims. For most of the 19th century, the connection between the Tsangpo of Tibet and the Brahmaputra of India was far from certain and subject to heated debate. It was well known that the Tsangpo flowed eastward a thousand miles across Tibet and disappeared into the knot of mountains at the Himalaya's eastern terminus. On the other side of *terra incognita*, five of Asia's great rivers flowed out within 200 miles of each other: the Yangtze, Mekong, Salween, Irrawaddy, and Brahmaputra. Even after the fact was generally accepted early in the 20th century that the Brahmaputra was fed by the Tsangpo, speculation remained about what happened between where the Tsangpo disappeared at roughly 9,000 feet of elevation and where it emerged at almost sea level in Assam. Did the mountain fastness conceal waterfalls to dwarf Niagara, or perhaps Victoria Falls on the Zambezi?

These wonderful questions, their answers guarded by implacable politics, impenetrable terrain, and intolerable weather, drew a worthy series of explorers: Pundits (native Indians recruited and trained by the Royal Trigonometrical Survey of the British Raj to conduct clandestine surveys in forbidden territories, as immortalized in Rudyard Kipling's novel *Kim*), British officers, an eccentric plant hunter accompanied by a Scottish Lord, a veteran Everest climber, and even a self-proclaimed reincarnation of Sir Richard Burton.

We know that the great 19th-century questions have been answered by a combination of classic exploration and modern satellite imagery. We now know that the Tsangpo gorges hold no thousand-foot waterfall (although a hundred-foot-high one was photographed and measured for the first time in late 1998). But as the 21st century begins, challenges remain in a dozen disciplines of field science and sport. And to this day, no one has succeeded, by any means, in completely traversing the gorges from one end to the other.

The massive uplift of the Himalaya and the Tibetan Plateau is caused by the collision of tectonic plates, as the Indian-Australian plate slams into and under the Eurasian continent, raising the former seacoast of the ancient Tethys Ocean tens of thousands of feet into the air. No mere curiosity of the geologic past, the uplift continues to this day at a rate some estimate to be as much as 10 millimeters per year. The eastern corner of this 1,500-mile-wide spade digging under Asia is one of the most active seismic zones on Earth, a rare place where one of nature's most awesome processes is visible, where the geologist can touch one giant landmass with his left hand and another with his right. Yet, it remains almost as unknown as a deep oceanic trench. All that it might reveal about plate tectonics is reserved for 21st-century geophysicists.

The ecology of the region is as special as the geology. The same break in the Himalayan massif that allows the Tsangpo River to flow down to the Assam plain allows a counterflow of moisture-laden monsoon air to ascend from the Bay of Bengal. Water vapor condenses with altitude to create the cloud forest, thousands of square miles of old-growth temperate rain forest. As elevation increases, bamboo thickets give way to steep slopes covered with tangles of rhododendron, saxifrage, primula, and orchids of dozens of species; cypress and other ancient trees hundreds of feet high; alpine meadows and bogs; and finally the arctic zone of the high glaciers.

Sheltered and nourished within this vast cloud forest are Himalayan bears, snow leopards and other hunting cats, red pandas, monkeys, and a rare wild bovine, the takin. More migratory bird species are found here than anywhere else in Asia. Snakes and leeches abound in variety and numbers to satisfy the most lurid adventure writer.

Human presence in the gorges is sparse but ancient. Buddhism, Bon, and animism coexist in villages that perch on shelves on the mountain slopes and practice slash-and-burn agriculture, some animal husbandry, and (rare in a Buddhist land) a hunting economy centered on the wild takin. Monpa tribes that have migrated from Bhutan mix with Lopas (Abors) from the hills of Assam as well as Tibetans. Strange tales circulate of a phallic cult and of a poison cult whose practitioners kill visitors with poisoned fingernails.

The mountains will of course endure, but the fate of the magnificent forest, and of the known and unknown species and cultures it nourishes, remains a test of the stewardship of Tibet, of China, and of the world.

In the midst of so many superlatives, statistics seem pedantic. However, there is a dramatic point within the roughly 140-mile-long series of gorges where the river flows directly between, and more than 16,000 feet below, the peaks of Namcha Barwa (25,446 feet) and Gyala Pelri (23,461 feet). By comparison, the Grand Canyon of the Colorado is only a fourth as deep. The Tsangpo carries a much greater volume of water than the Colorado River and has a gradient many times steeper, making both rapids and land travel incomparably more difficult.

ON SEPTEMBER 28, THREE DAYS OUT OF KATHMANDU and just short of Lhasa, the vehicles arrived at a much anticipated and portentous landmark, a long highway bridge over the Tsangpo. We had reached the river that had been in our dreams and ambitions for as long as 15 years, and it would consume every waking thought and ounce of energy for the next several weeks.

Green-fatigued Chinese soldiers sporting the red star of the Peoples Liberation Army stirred anxiously as our three Land Cruisers pulled up to the bridge's southern abutment and we eagerly spilled out to begin examining the surroundings. Their concern abated somewhat when it became clear that we were foreigners, not high-ranking military or civil officers (the only others who would be driving in such luxurious vehicles). On simultaneous suggestions from Paulo and me, members of our group ostentatiously put their cameras back into the cars, and the soldiers visibly relaxed and paid us no further mind. We were evidently tourists, not spies; in any case, we knew and followed the rules.

Still roughly 300 miles upstream from our destination, the Tsangpo flowed wide and flat between dun-colored bluffs of sedimentary deposits. Sand beaches and islands punctuated the swift gray water, rafts and yak-hide coracles ferried across the stiller pools, and the topography gave no hint of the steep gorges to come. Yet this look at the river was of enormous importance, because it would begin to answer a fundamental question that had been the source of concern and speculation since long before we departed the United States.

MASSIVE FLOODS HAD ENGULFED CHINA, TIBET, and Bangladesh during the summer of 1998 and were the subject of conflicting reports and rumors. Before departure we had heard the July and August flooding on China's Yangtze reported as "50-year floods," while the flood in Bangladesh (the ultimate destination of the Tsangpo/ Brahmaputra) was called the longest in duration for decades. But the Chinese do not publish flow data of their rivers as is done in the West, and they are often defensive and secretive about natural disasters. Thus, even our knowledge of average expected flows was fragmentary, and although we knew that the floods and the Indian summer monsoon were over, accurate information about how quickly the water was dropping and what we would encounter in October and November could come only through personal observation.

The rate of flow in a river (cubic feet per second in America or cubic meters per second in Europe) is of fundamental importance to white-water paddlers. Two factors are generally considered to be in a roughly inverse relationship: The greater the flow, the less steep the river must be for any given level of difficulty. Thus a creek flowing at only a few hundred cubic feet per second may be run while dropping more than 200 feet per mile; the Colorado River, on average, drops only 8 feet per mile in the Grand Canyon, but it flows at 10,000 to 30,000 or more cubic feet per second.

Another factor that is even more subjective, but nevertheless critical, is the relationship of the flow to the norm for the particular river, to the bed that the river has carved for itself over centuries of seeking the path of least resistance. In a river near or beyond its flood stage—"bank full"—the flow of water in the overloaded channel becomes more turbulent, less predictable, more powerful, and more dangerous. In a river at minimum flow, water sifts through the rock-filled bed, channels run completely under piles of boulders, and drops are steep and congested; getting pinned on the rocks becomes the danger. Somewhere in between is the white-water paddler's hoped-for median.

How these factors apply on Himalayan rivers, which have huge high-water flows part of the year and are locked in ice the remainder, remains to be learned in this young sport. Our first view of the Tsangpo was both intimidating and hopeful. The river was immense, gray with suspended sediment, hundreds of yards in width. No doubt there was considerably more water than Tom and I had observed the previous year, even though we were hundreds of miles upstream. Yet, every sign on the river indicated rapidly falling water levels. Series of little vertical steps in the damp sand of each beach indicated daily drops. When the sand dried completely, it would crumble into an even slope, so rising or stable water levels would have shown a smoother gradient.

From a single view in a relatively flat stretch of river, we were unable even to estimate the total flow, nor could we tell the rate at which the level was dropping. We now knew part of the equation, but exactly what we would encounter days and weeks later, with greatly different topography, required more data. Whether the river team could even put their boats in the water was in doubt.

IN THE STATES BY PHONE AND E-MAIL, on the plane and in Kathmandu, we had considered our options. While it was always possible to give up the idea entirely or to delay for a more favorable year, these options were distasteful for a number of reasons besides the obvious, that we were eager to confront the Tsangpo's magnificent challenge. Starting over would not be easy. Given the vagaries of Chinese politics and Tibetan policy, duplication of our fortunately obtained permits would be a gamble. The authorities could easily close the region entirely, or they could, given greatly increased interest from both Chinese and other international river teams, place this in the category of major climbing expeditions and demand huge permit fees. For the first ascent of Namcha Barwa, Japanese climbers reputedly paid a million dollars while for the first rafting descent of the Yangtze, Oregonian Ken Warren negotiated down to a mere $300,000.

Restructuring would present both psychological and practical problems as well. Maintaining the same team composition for yet another long absence from families and careers would likely be impossible. Rebuilding the financial base and sponsorship would also be difficult. By July, before the first hints of floods, we had committed roughly $50,000 for permits,—for specifically named individuals to travel in specific areas within specified dates—vehicle transport, and related travel services during the expedition. Authorities in Tibet were unlikely to consider our dissatisfaction with the weather grounds for refund.

Without exception, in our experience, sponsors and supporters of difficult expeditions understand the risky nature of these undertakings and are scrupulously careful not to influence decision-making. There is, however, a self-imposed element of pride and sense of obligation associated with an effort of this magnitude—obligations to teammates, to the sport, and to those who have supported the effort with endorsements, equipment, or funds. Tom and I (and, to a lesser extent, Jamie) had learned a hard lesson nearly 25 years before.

SHORTLY AFTER THE MUNICH GAMES, on the wave of elation and confidence created by the sport's first Olympic effort, we asked ourselves what should happen next. Our ambitious conclusion was that white-water kayaking should follow the example set by mountaineers 50 years before, graduating from the Alps to the Himalaya. We were not alone. Unknown to us until we began our research and planning, Hans Memminger and a German team had run the Kali Gandaki River in Nepal in 1971 and were soon to be followed by others. By 1975, Mike Jones in England was paralleling our planning steps as he put together a pioneering descent of the Dudh Kosi on Everest.

East of Nepal, the classic "forbidden kingdom" of Bhutan was just beginning to emerge from centuries of isolation. Under its young king, Jigme Wangchuk, a few foreign travelers were allowed into limited areas beginning in 1972, exposing the nation gradually to the modern world. No expeditions—

scientific, climbing, or, of course, whitewater—had yet been admitted, and Bhutan remained a pristine example of medieval Buddhist culture, as Tibet must have been before invasion by the Chinese in early October of 1950. In 1975 Tom and I therefore concluded that Bhutan was a worthy goal. As long as we were mounting a costly expedition to run unexplored rivers halfway around the world, the extra difficulty in gaining admission to Bhutan would be amply repaid by the opportunity to practice our craft in so wonderful a setting. This decision was ultimately accurate, but it was to lead to five years of frustrating delays and acute embarrassment before our peers.

Initial reaction by Bhutanese officials was encouraging, although it was clear that our ambitions went well beyond their fledgling tourist program and fulfilling them would require special permission from the king. We forged ahead with plans, perhaps underestimating in our optimism just how difficult getting special exceptions would be.

We also made a second decision that would prove costly to our pride. Because the concept of expedition paddling was new, and an idea we wanted to promote, we felt justified in asking for support and financial contributions from the paddling community. We made the rounds of paddling clubs, selling T-shirts and decals, promising slide shows upon our return, and sending out a monthly newsletter about our plans and progress to every contributor.

By July 1976 we had raised enough money for airplane fares, obtained mountains of equipment from manufacturers, and enlisted a promise of support from National Geographic magazine. By August, in excited anticipation, we were stuffing our boats full of gear and rations for the flight. But by September we were ruefully unpacking and putting everything into long-term storage at Tom's summer camp outside Washington, D.C. Not all of the expected special permissions had been granted. What would be allowed was both beyond our budget and far short of the route down the Wong Chu River we had set as our goal.

Five years later, the Bhutanese were somewhat more liberal toward travelers. And five years older, we were somewhat less dogmatic in telling the King of Bhutan exactly how, where, and for how long expeditions should be conducted in his country. As we slid our boats into Himalayan water for the first time, in October 1981. and drifted under the prayer-flag-festooned bridges of Thimphu, I wondered about our reasons for being there.[3] How much of this journey was for the pure love of adventure, and how much resulted from stubbornness, after five years of explaining to every paddler we met what had happened to all the grand plans we had boasted about?

THAT HISTORY WAS PART OF OUR CALCULATION, along with modern considerations, as we early determined to take advantage of whatever opportunity we had in hand in 1998 to achieve as much as we prudently could. If, in the end, boating in the gorges proved beyond the limits of manageable risk. then we would conduct a world-class foot reconnaissance, either for our own future use or as a leg up for other expeditions.

That unpalatable option, and giving up their special goal of paddling the Tsangpo, would of course be hardest on the river team, and there was no immediate concensus among the four about the choice. From their first view of the swollen river at the road bridge onward, Tom decided that the river team would ride in a single Land Cruiser, where they could observe, discuss, make plans, and coalesce as a team on a continuous basis. None of them realized that their efforts to talk over the noise of the engine, passing traffic, and the driver's Chinese rock tape was a rehearsal for learning to communicate over the unceasing din of the loudest river they had ever encountered.

CHAPTER 3

BIG
WATER

We [are] but pygmies... lost among the boulders.[1]

—MAJOR JOHN WESLEY POWELL

FTER YEARS OF ANTICIPATION and speculation about the Tsangpo River, and months of rumor and anxiety concerning the floods, finally at Pei the paddlers had hard facts and cold water to test. With relief they put behind them the thirteen days of fatiguing travel, the spilled kerosene, the misplaced batteries, the light-fingered porters, and even the yaks and Buddhist monasteries, the exotic streets of Lhasa, and the snowy passes crowned with prayer flags. Those things and more would be savored later as the backdrop to the adventure. For the moment they were but distractions in the serious business of paddling.

From road's end at the village of Pei, to Gyala, the last

village at the upstream end of the gorges, the river rehearses for its plunge to the Indian plain more than 9,000 feet below. For roughly 15 miles, rapids are large but spaced apart, the average gradient a fraction of the continuous drop downstream. A trail parallels the river's course, high on the bluffs above the right bank. Here, with resupply close at hand and a ready exit route if necessary, the paddlers were to test their equipment, adjust to the river as individual athletes and as a team, and ultimately decide whether and how they could proceed beyond.

The four donned waterproof nylon dry suits, latex cuffs and collars almost uncomfortably tight at the ankles, wrists, and neck, and pulled neoprene spray skirts up to seal around their waists. Snugging themselves into the bracing of their boats, they stretched the lower ends of the spray skirts taut over cockpit rims to complete their waterproof seal, and eagerly tipped forward off a steep embankment of gray, micaceous silt to slither like otters down 20 feet into the cold water.

Below the towering peaks of Namcha Barwa and Gyala Pelri, with every point of reference drawn to the same unimaginable scale, the Tsangpo appeared to the paddlers like many a large river they had seen in the Alps or the Canadian Rockies: swiftly flowing flats embroidered with the lace of periodic rapids. But rapids that looked easy from trails a thousand feet above, and still looked not too difficult from shore, proved to have shocking power and velocity when actually run. Trains of big haystack waves in the center of the current rose twenty or more feet from trough to crest, and when their surging crests broke over like combers on a stormy sea, the tumbling wall of white could engulf a kayak, halt all downstream momentum, and threw boat and boater back down into the trough. As Doug would learn in the very first rapid, only when the breaking waves relented could a kayak survive the center line of the rapids.

More dangerously, where the rocketing current flowed over underwater boulders or bedrock ledges, huge holes were formed: recirculating backwashes downstream of the obstacles. All rapids have holes. Kayaks and rafts crash through the smaller ones with impunity; kayakers play and surf and hold rodeo competitions on the white flow of moderate-size ones. But those on the Tsangpo were immense, unnavigable, and deadly, the biggest 20 verticle feet in height and stretching more than a hundred feet across the river's width. Their circular flow would snatch up and recirculate a boat and paddler, and, unlike the pulsing, breaking waves, their steady, violent recircualtion could tumble a boat, or log, or any floating object for uncalculable lengths of time.

Before launching into any rapid, the paddlers had to identify a clean line or route of downstream current that would avoid the biggest of the exploding waves and all of the angry holes. Then, once on the surging flow, blinded intermittently by crashing spray and able to see their surroundings for only seconds at a time as they crested the six to ten foot waves, they had to power their laden boats unerringly down the chosen route.

ON OCTOBER 5, 1998, JAMIE MCEWAN WROTE in his journal:
>...*the water picks up right away and starts rocking us in long smooth undulations. You can feel that it's deep, underneath us. You can feel the latent power...*

When I reach the middle of the river I turn down, pick up speed. I can see the tops of the waves, see them shift and roll and spurt plumes of spray. The raw brute power of it. I hear them as one great massive sound, with occasional extra-loud pops and booms.

I'm heading straight for a crashing wave mid-river. It's one of hundreds of waves we ignored, when we scouted; they seemed so small, and so easy to avoid, in the wide channel. Now the wave seems to grow, both taller and wider, and to be crawling upstream at me as I am swept down toward it. I can hear it, too; I can pick out the sound of that specific wave. It must be taller than my head. And breaking, constantly breaking....

Okay, I'm intimidated. Instinctively I turn aside, go left; I can avoid the main power there...but I've put half the river between myself and the others.

A pour-over hole goes by on my left, giving off a side wave that throws my bow up and out of control for one shocking half-second. Regaining my balance, I turn straight downstream. Another hole roars by, and now, below me, I can see the big inviting eddy against the left shore. I focus there, blinking and shaking off each wave, break through a head-high last wave that somewhere off to my right grows monstrous, and sizzle into the eddy.

Here I rest. Breathe. I'm perfectly safe, behind the eddy fence, though the mad waves are booming at me, their spray filling the air. I am over the drop; I could, if I choose, slip down the left side without challenging them. Crossing to the other side will be another matter. But I am down. I am whole. The sun shines up where it should.

I climb out to take pictures, but before I have time to set up I catch a flash of blue and realize that I am seeing a boat. My god it's tiny! Maybe a quarter the size that I'd been looking for. Crossing my way, toward river left, a yellow helmet: Doug.

When he reaches mid-river he turns downstream... He disappears behind a "small" entrance wave, rises up again; blades flashing, he charges down the last long slope, drops into the wave that's rolling right there across from me.

The wave swallows him: opens up, invites him in, closes down again. Boat, paddle, helmet, gone. I see nothing but water. We hadn't thought of this wave as a "keeper" because it's not constantly breaking; there are moments when it smoothes out and shouldn't hold anything.

But now, perversely, it just breaks and breaks and breaks.

The seconds thud by. Brief flashes of blue come and go in the maelstrom, like a single blue sock in the suds of an off-white load. I keep looking downstream, convinced that I have missed Doug's washing out, only to realize he is still in there.

Finally I see his blue boat float clear, hull up. He's been held for so long that I assume that, desperate for air, he has kicked free of his boat, or soon will, but no, his paddle appears on the surface, the boat twists as he tries to roll. I'm surprised when he fails. I can count the times I have seen Doug fail to roll on the fingers of one hand—and I have seen him succeed hundreds. The next wave crashes on him, smothering his next attempt: bad timing. Now, surely, he'll come out. But no again; on the far side of the wave, well downstream of me now, he tries once more, and this time, slowly, awkwardly, he puts the boat under him.

Even the smaller waves below are big enough that he keeps disappearing and reappearing as he paddles over to the far bank. Once there he rests, then waves a hand, probably to say that he is all right, though at that distance—the width of the river—I can't be sure. And I don't think I would hear him over the sound of the rapid if he set off a stick of dynamite....

THE RIVER WAS, IN FACT, ENORMOUS—on a par with the biggest flows anyone on the team had ever attempted. Years before, Tom and I had run part of the Potomac's Mathur Gorge during hurricane floods of 70,000 cubic feet per second, and Jamie had run the Niagara Gorge at 100,000. This flow was less; team members estimated it anywhere between 20,000 and 45,000 cubic feet per second. But this was no short run of a few miles, and the gradient when the Tsangpo entered the canyon proper would be far steeper than those examples. One hopeful aspect was that the banks were built to the same gargantuan scale, fields of huge boulders and flood-scoured bedrock 30 and more feet above the present water level, perhaps offering alternative passage downstream.

The difficulty the paddlers experienced in appreciating true size and scale was anticipated, yet still they were deceived. The mind sees what experience leads it to expect, and mountaineers have long remarked that even the most veteran eye can be fooled by the unprecedented scale of the Himalaya. Legendary climber and explorer Eric Shipton described the early days of his landmark 1934 exploration of Nanda Devi with H.W. Tilman:

I found myself to be very nervous and shaky on the steep grass slopes and slabs on which we had to climb. This was due to the fact that I was not yet used to the immense scale of the gorge and its surroundings. Tilman suffered from the same complaint. We also had great difficulty in judging the size and angle of minor features. This made route-finding from a distance very difficult indeed, and we were continually finding ourselves in error. However, the eye gradually adjusted itself, and soon we began to move with more confidence. [2]

Sixty-five years later, Jamie commented in his own journal: *Surprising how we don't cease being surprised.*

ADJUSTMENT TO THE SCALE WAS NOT THE ONLY LESSON to be learned from mountaineering and other alpine sports. Modern whitewater racing was born in the alpine countries of Europe in the fifties and sixties, and from the beginning it was patterned after ski competition, divided into slalom and downriver, analogous to downhill skiing. River-runners and expedition paddlers similarly looked to the climbing world for models.

White-water sport was barely in its infancy when Tenzing Norgay and Edmund Hillary summited Everest, however, and the most valid comparison for expedition paddling in the Himalya is not modern mountaineering on Everest and other well-established major peaks, but to the mountaineering of roughly 50 years ago. Pioneers like George Mallory had made their marks and scores of lesser peaks had been climbed, but major peaks remained untouched. Eric Shipton and H.W.

Tilman struggled to discover access routes even to start climbing the 8,000-meter giants, while improvements in technique and equipment made the peaks tantalizingly more attainable year by year.

The techniques used by white-water teams to bypass unrunnable rapids also reflect the rock climbing methods of an earlier era. Although the most modern equipment is available to choose from, there are severe limits on what can be carried in the boats. Boaters are restricted to a very basic suite of equipment and to a single pair of general purpose shoes that must serve for paddling, swimming, and long-distance trekking as well as climbing. Lightweight, nonelastic rescue ropes must frequently serve as climbing rope, with performance much like that of obsolete hemp ropes. Body belays and similar archaic techniques still serve instead of modern specialized equipment. Even as the Tsangpo team worked their way through the first few miles of river, they debated their choice between a rudimentary "twelve pound" and a more robust "eighteen pound" kit of climbing gear.

Since its inception, white-water sport has grown exponentially. Fueled by the evolution of technique and of ever more durable, light, and high-performance equipment made of space-age plastics, each decade has seen a leap in the difficulty of rivers that are safely navigated. Whether the state of the art in 1998 was equal to what lay hidden within the Tsangpo gorges, however, would only be learned by trying, in the tradition of Mallory and Irvine, Shipton and Tilman, Hillary and Tenzing Norgay.

DOUG'S HUMBLING THRASHING in the very first rapid demonstrated that the four paddlers would have to make adjustments

to navigate the enormous Tsangpo's flow. All refined and
adjusted their boats and equipment; Doug tightened the bracing that held him solid in his boat and had no further trouble
snapping the boat upright with Eskimo rolls when needed.
Their eyes adjusted to see the water in its actual scale. Their leg
muscles became accustomed to traversing the slippery, rounded
boulders of the river's shore. And each night they discussed how
it might be in the steeper gorge itself, where the huge rapids
became so frequent that one merged into the next.

During this testing period, Harry and Doris Wetherbee,
Paulo Castillo and Pemba Sherpa trekked slowly down to
Gyala, available to assist, rescue if necessary, and resupply the
paddlers for their plunge into the gorge below if they elected
to go on. Simultaneously, Dave Phillips and I, accompanied by
Ang Kami Sherpa, had already separated from the group, and
were following another road to loop around to the north. From
a foot trail leading into the heart of the gorge, we were to work
our way in advance of the paddlers to the first resupply point,
roughly 27 miles downstream from Gyala in the vicinity of
Rainbow Falls.

For a total of eight days, the paddlers slowly worked their
way downstream from Pei, spending more time on foot than in
the boats, painstakingly scouting each drop. They carried or
dragged the boats back upstream to run rapids multiple times.
Because this was a full rehearsal for the challenges ahead, their
boats carried all the gear and several days supply of food. They
had trained all summer with extra weight in their boats at home.
Now they became accustomed to paddling, and stumbling along
the boulder fields ashore, with the specific 90- to 100-pound
combination of boat and gear that they would depend upon,

and curse, for the duration of the expedition. At night they bivouacked near the shore, testing each item of camp gear and experimenting to lighten the load, ounce by jealous ounce.

The critical link by satellite telephone to the rest of the expedition was exercised, even though one support party was often just out of reach. As with all communications systems under difficult circumstances, this proved trickier in practice than in theory. Contrary to all known laws of physics and electronics, the satellite phone that Tom carried on the river refused to link with mine, although both phones reliably reached Harry Wetherbee. As long as that held true, Harry could relay essential messages. If that link failed, we would have to use the much less flexible alternative of preplanned meeting points, with elaborate fallback plans for the inevitable contingencies.

On the evening of October 6, from their first bivouac site by the river, Tom tested the satellite telephone by summarizing the expedition's start for Renee Montagne at National Public Radio's Radio Expeditions, a partner with the National Geographic Society. Transmitted with difficulty over the constant din of the nearby river, his efforts to report with perfect accuracy and in terms intelligible to the general, drive-time public understandably reflected little of a locale so exotic, a landscape so immense, and a test so difficult even the participants had a hard time comprehending.

> MONTAGNE: *"Now, am I right that you are start-ing the trip today?"*
> TOM: *"Actually it's taken us about 13 days to travel to the river across Tibet from Kathmandu, Nepal."*
> MONTAGNE: *"And what lies ahead, then,*

in the next few miles?"

TOM: *"There are enormous rapids around every turn of the river. And we are actually paddling the margins along the shore and catching the small eddies to try to stay out of the huge power of this river."*

MONTAGNE: *"And you'll be kayaking the entire river?"*

TOM: *"We're going to kayak as much of it as we can. It's still uncertain how much we'll be able to kayak. We haven't seen all of the river, and we're exploring as we go."*

MONTAGNE: *"You talked about rapids. What makes this river so tough? Why tougher than any other rapids that you've encountered?"*

TOM: *"Well, the volume of water going down the river is...somewhere in the range of 20,000 cubic feet per second, maybe up to 35,000 cubic feet per second, which is enormous....like the Potomac in very high, almost flood.... And that is already, we have found, a difficult and slightly dangerous situation."*

MONTAGNE: *"And what was that?"*

TOM: *"Oh, huge crashing waves...in the middle of the river....And we still have to do a considerable amount of scouting on foot because we can't really go down a river or down a rapid without actually seeing what's ahead. So we hike to around the corners and down along the shores...just to figure out what the best course of action will be."*

MONTAGNE: *"We will be checking in with you again as you traverse the Tsangpo River in the coming*

couple of months. Take care of yourself."
TOM: *"We certainly will. We're trying."*

THE FOLLOWING MORNING FOUND THE TEAM SPLIT as they bypassed a violent rapid down the left bank, experimenting to discover the most efficient methods to traverse the river's banks. Doug Gordon and Roger Zbel roped their way up a cliff and proceeded slowly along a "high road," while Tom and Jamie picked their way through the jumble of gigantic boulders and narrow side channels at water level.

The brothers became entirely absorbed in their three-dimensional boulder labyrinth. To avoid lifting the heavily loaded boats, they slid them up steep rocks, wedged them in like gigantic pitons, and climbed up using the cockpit rims and nylon grab loops on either end as handholds. At each apex, they hauled the boats up to balance, then slid them down the other side. Sometimes they leaped into chest-deep pools, the water pouring into their unzipped dry suits a welcome relief from the hot labor. Occasionally they could paddle short distances, down steep, almost dry side channels.

Sign language was often more useful than trying to shout over the hungry roar of the rapid out of sight to their right. The silent, laborious teamwork as they made their way downstream was companionable: A bond was somehow easier for the two intense brothers to achieve by traveling halfway around the globe and challenging the world's most difficult white water than it was during the course of their daily lives in Maryland and Connecticut.

The previous day, Tom had noticed Jamie taking pictures from shore and had halted, unasked, in the next eddy to wait for him. Several minutes went by while Jamie repacked his gear into its waterproof bag and carefully clambered in, but Tom did not turn down until Jamie paddled alongside. The immense landscape imposes a sense of isolation and human frailty, and as their two boats flushed down the last part of the rapid almost side by side, Jamie felt a profound appreciation for this simple, thoughtful act. Neither brother had spoken.

Emerging at last from the rocky maze, they came to a major channel. Unlike the tiny "creeks" above, this started as a moderate stream, melded for a moment with the main river, and split left again at a towering boulder to become a small river of its own, flowing down the shore and over a final decisive slide of six or eight feet. The only apparent difficulty was the lack of a good way to enter the water. For on the huge, turbulent Tsangpo, even eddies of water behind rocks and along the shorelines were not still pools, but surging caldrons that pulsed up and down three and more feet, like waves rolling into a rocky beach. Whirlpools formed, skittered across the water, and disappeared, and mushroom shaped boils loomed up from the depths, some more than twice a boat length across, water flowing powerfully from the upwelling and center in all directions to the edges. It was difficult enough to paddle in the midst of this turbulence when fully set in the boat; sliding into a tippy kayak and sealing the watertight sprayskirt in the violence was out of the question. Almost invariably the paddlers were forced to get set in their boats on a dry rock above the roiling water, then slide or tumble down into the river in what was called a "seal launch." Tom got into his boat perched on a sloping ledge of rock, then slid awkwardly into the stream. With a quick brace he regained his balance; a smooth series of strokes guided him confidently around the corner and over the slide, to disappear into an eddy below.

Selecting instead a narrow, flat-topped block of black-and-white gneiss for his launching platform, Jamie balanced his boat on top, checked his dry-suit zipper, life-jacket ties, and helmet buckle. With his paddle teetering across the deck just in front of his body, he reached behind and secured his neoprene spray skirt under the lip of the cockpit rim behind his back. Leaving the sides for last, he reached forward to repeat the process in front.

Suddenly, as his weight shifted imperceptibly forward, gravity took command, man's will no longer relevant. With a grind and a thump, the boat pitched forward into the water. Releasing the unsecured spray skirt to seize his all-important paddle, Jamie braced the boat upright and pointed it downstream, but as he did so he felt the first surge of water pour into the open cockpit against his right leg. With each succeeding wave, the boat took on more water and became less responsive to its occupant. The stern sank into each swirl of current; the bow waved uncontrollably in the air.

Then the boat flipped entirely, and as Jamie rolled it upright (now completely full, a sea anchor of several hundred pounds almost completely unsteerable in the current) he saw directly ahead the last towering boulder dividing the flow, separating side channel from main river. If he could only get left of that rock, into the side chute, everything would be fine. He would arrive in the big eddy below, and Tom would be there. They would pick up the pieces and laugh it off.

Washing closer, trying desperately to push the unstable, leaden boat to the left, Jamie noticed an ominous detail. With only seconds to react, his vision blurred by water still draining from his helmet after the Eskimo roll, he could see that the upstream end of the boulder did not feature the usual cushion of piled-up water, the bow wave that washes objects to one side or the other. The water instead flowed smoothly under; the rock was undercut, the most dangerous situation in white water. The next time the boat lurched to its side he let it tip, and then he kicked out and away from the boat, to the right of the rock pillar that threatened to engulf him.

A wave passed over Jamie's head, murky water obscured the sunlight, and strangely he felt himself relax. After the desperate flurry of activity trying to save the situation, in an instant his responsibilities were almost nil. Flotsam goes where the river dictates. His job now was simply to breathe: Feeling the rhythm of the waves, he breathed deeply as he was thrown upward and tried not to choke as water rolled overhead. Fear remained, of course. As he rose to sunlight, he could see that he was in the main river, on the left edge of the flow. A long train of waves crested up and toward him, and sliding down the next pitch he could feel his stomach rise. One breath, and he was under again.

"Take my stern! Grab hold!" His brother's shouted commands caught Jamie's attention. He saw the bright blue of Tom's kayak and grabbed the yellow loop on its stern. Without pause in his slow, powerful strokes toward shore, Tom looked back over his shoulder, glasses flashing: "Are you all right? Are you cold?"

Despite Jamie's entreaties for Tom to look immediately for the lost boat while Jamie swam unassisted to shore, Tom hovered close for a moment in seeming indecision, knowing that in cases of injury or hypothermia, the victim is often the last to recognize the seriousness of the situation. Finally Tom paddled down the eddy, as Jamie, using his paddle as a staff, climbed out onto the gravel beach. He sat, gazing downstream for his boat as water drained from his sodden gear.

But Tom turned back at the base of the eddy. They had not scouted farther, and on this river going around blind corners was not to be contemplated for any reason, least of all simply to retrieve gear. Jamie would have to walk out.

He would later record:

> They pump me up as best they can: pat me on the back, shit happens, maybe we'll find it, it's all part of the adventure, don't worry about it. . . . Despite the pumping it's a pretty dejected Jamie who climbs upslope. . . . I carry my paddle. I'm weighted, too, with guilt, feelings of inadequacy. I've let my compadres down; I've marred our plan. We had chosen to bring four paddlers for good reasons: partly for safety, partly to spread out the "group gear" like stove, cameras, and satellite phone.
>
> How could I have slipped? How could I choose the wrong spot like that? Maybe I should have held onto the boat when I swam.
>
> Well below me, five or seven hundred vertical feet or more (surprisingly far, for I don't feel that I have climbed very high—or is the river really dropping fast enough to matter?) runs the rippled water. The cliff goes on above me at least that far again. Out in the air before me fly a group of five or six birds, tumbling and climbing. Glaciers appear and disappear in the distant sky. Everything is so big, outsized, it makes you feel not so much small as fragile, and also precious.

There are little bugs on the river's surface. Colored
bugs. Three of them. I sit, watch. They pull toward shore,
disembark on a mixed rock and sand beach. . . . In min-
utes the walkie-talkie radio comes alive, and I hear the bug
down below that is Doug.

"River team to Jamie. River team to Jamie. Come in
please."

"Hiker to river team. I can see you."

TWO SWEATY HOURS LATER, HIGH ABOVE THE LEFT BANK of the river,
Jamie spotted little "bugs" on the rippled surface below, three
bright red-and-blue bugs that scooted to the opposite shore, dis-
embarked on a rock-and-sand beach, and began to build a
bivouac camp. Jamie disconsolately returned to his footpath,
berating himself for the instant of inattention that had cost him
his boat and thus cut him off from his brother, his teammates,
and his part in the long-dreamed-of expedition. Sourly he
reflected that downstream with the boat had gone his carefully
kept journal, his camera, and his exposed film, also robbing him
of part of what he had accomplished so far.

Even in a land where yetis are considered a natural part of
the ecosystem and lamas are supposed to levitate from one
monastery to another at will, Jamie McEwan must have
appeared exotic: He was six feet tall, with black hair and the
stubble of an emerging beard on a jutting chin. He had flashing dark eyes and was more Celtic in appearance than his
brother, and more fey. He wore his cobalt blue dry suit unzipped,
its arms tied around his waist, topped with a lime green long
underwear top and yellow life jacket; his walking stick was a
black carbon-fiber canoe paddle spiraled with white and black

tape. But Buddhism teaches a serene acceptance of all life's strange manifestations, natural and supernatural. Villagers would halt their plowing teams of yaks or pause from parching great pans of corn over smoky fires to contemplate briefly the stranger stalking down the path, and then they would silently return to their labors or speak politely and uncuriously. Pilgrims, as we had noted in the teeming streets of Lhasa, come in all shapes and costumes.

The trail coursed alternately up and down the steep hillside, seeking purchase on a slope that yielded it only reluctantly. Brief, tantalizing stretches of good path, occasionally even revealing the double ruts of wheeled vehicles and at one rocky corner the obvious product of blasting, inevitably bifurcated into confusing braids of animal tracks. Sometimes the way was blocked by gates of wooden poles, sometimes by the zo (a hybrid cross of yak and cattle) the gates were placed to contain. Jamie later recorded:

> In the quieter stretches, where the sound of the rapids fades to a steady roar, I can faintly hear my own footfalls. Pat, pat, pat, my light river shoes on the rocks. Rarely do I hear anything else. Insects, sometimes: a sound similar to our cicadas, yet different, as if they too speak Tibetan. More rarely, a bird call. Mostly roar, and the pats of my own shoes.
>
> ...The sun stands, amongst scattered clouds, above and behind the big wooded hills that back the plateau. Its rays pick out the tops of the taller trees, outlines the wrinkles of side ridges, all against the darker background of shadowed slopes. The river is invisible, buried off to my right. The plateau before me seems spotlighted, highlighted by the

slanting rays. As if I were stepping out of shadowed wings
onto the real stage.

Dusk fell, then total darkness. Hours earlier Jamie had been confident of reaching the ferry that crosses a flat stretch of the river at Gyala before dark. Now he had no idea how far he had come, and the last Tibetan he had encountered had responded to his query by carefully tracing four full circuits of Jamie's watch dial with a dirty fingernail. But Jamie had not maintained his place on the U.S. Whitewater Team for more than 20 years, including two Olympic games, and followed his medal at Munich with a fourth-place finish a full 20 years later at the Barcelona Games, by being passive in the face of adversity. His reaction now was to assuage his frustration with physical effort, the harder the better, and to continue progress in the direction his boat had disappeared. Whether this was in the scant hope of recovery, or in penance for his error, he could not tell.

Insects and what sounded exactly like Maryland tree frogs were in full evening chorus as Jamie angled upward through thick brush, searching for clues to the elusive trail by looking for openings in the vegetation silhouetted against the night sky. Twigs and dirt worked their way inside his unzipped dry suit, and his helmet caught repeatedly in the bushes until he put it on, at which time sweat began to pour into his eyes. Once he laughed out loud, thinking sardonically: "Behold the great Himalayan explorer." It was a spooky sound, though, and he did not repeat it.

Light-headed and slightly dizzy from trying to keep his balance in the darkness, he rested for a moment, leaning an arm on a tree and putting his head on the inside of that elbow for stability. Briefly he considered admitting defeat, starting a fire with the lighter Roger had equipped him with before they separated, and sleeping right on the trail. He had been without water since before night fell, however, so he pushed on to find at least a side stream.

Finally the moon appeared, jumping from cloud to cloud, and the faint trace of a path was again discernible. Suddenly, shockingly, from the trail ahead came voices and a shout Jamie belatedly recognized as his own name in young Pemba Sherpa's accented English.

Two hours later he wearily followed the firefly lead of the search party's flashlight, zigzagging down beside a gushing stream to a sandy beach. The light of a driftwood bonfire flickered off the swift but flat, immensely wide, and strangely silent river and revealed the dark faces of an old piratical-looking ferryman and his two assistants, along with the tall, familiar, reassuring figure of Harry Wetherbee. It was 2:00 a.m.

With dazed wonder Jamie watched as the three river pirates started up the old truck engine set in the back of their barge-like ferry; the long, esoteric process involved, at one point, dramatically thrusting a flaming kerosene-soaked torch into the guts of the machine. On the far shore was the temporary support base Harry had established at Gyala, with tent, food, spare clothes, and supportive companions.

All this was welcome, but it was no mitigation of Jamie's frustration over the loss of his place with the river team, nor of his nagging, irrational guilt over somehow letting the others down. He drifted off to sleep inside his tent, wearing all his extra clothes inside a spare Gore-Tex® bivouac sack—there was no extra sleeping bag—and listening to the roar of the kerosene stove as Pemba Sherpa cooked himself a long-delayed dinner.

CHAPTER 4

SUPPORT SYSTEMS

*Sir, –The Lama who was sent with me sold me
to a Jongpon as a slave…. on account of which
the journey proved a bad one….*

—KINTHUP

NSIDE A LARGE black-and-yellow expedition
tent, obtained specifically to accommodate
base-camp operations (and six-foot-three-
inch base-camp operators), Harry Wetherbee
stretched out his chronically painful back. Jamie's turnabout of
fortune was devastating, he reflected, but hardly unprecedented
in the exploration of remote reaches of Asia. This he knew both
from personal experience and from the region's history, for the
lodestar that drew Harry and Doris to their roles in support of
the river team was not the lifetime obsession that the four paddlers and I had with rivers around the globe. Rather, theirs was
an equal fascination with the byways, peoples, smells, sounds,
and history of Central and South Asia.

Seven years earlier and 1,200 miles west of the Tsangpo gorges, Harry, Doris, and I had stood, shivering despite strong sunlight, and gazed around at the brown and green, tundra-clad rolling slopes of the Khunjerab Pass on the crest of the Karakoram. Neither altitude headaches nor the breathlessness from standing at 18,000 feet of elevation could dull our sense of romance. Directly behind us lay the fabulous, snow-curtained Hunza Valley, aimed like an immense avalanche chute down to the Indus Valley and the verdant heart of the Indian subcontinent beyond. Ahead lay the vast, barren steppes of Central Asia, the Taklimakan and Gobi deserts, and the legendary cities of the Silk Road. Kashgar and Yarkant were closest, Turfan beyond to the north and east, Bokhara and Samarkand to the then still forbidden west.

At once well-publicized and mysterious, Central Asia has been traversed since ancient times by traders like Marco Polo, and warriors like Gengis Khan and Tamerlane. Yet its depths have never been a goal easily achieved. In the 19th century this became the arena for that century's cold war: "The Great Game" of Rudyard Kipling and his contemporaries of the British Raj in India; "The Tournament of Shadows" to the officers and agents of Tsarist Russia.

By the second half of the 19th century, the expanding Tsarist empire had brutally subdued the tribes of the Caucasus, including modern Chechnya and Dagestan, and was reaching hungrily for the ancient Muslim city-states of Central Asia. Ahead of the Cossack forces roved scouts, surveyors, and spies, learning the terrain, seeking alliances, playing one khan against another to the ultimate subjugation of both.

Far to the south and east, men who had done much the same

to the princely states of India considered, with growing unease, the dwindling buffer between the empires. The Indian subcontinent lay beyond the most daunting natural fortifications on the planet. The center was held by the great arcing Himalaya, more than 1,200 miles in length and up to more than 29,000 feet high. The flanks, where the ranges gradually descended into more humanly scaled hills and valleys, were no less formidable. The barren rocky hills and mountains of the Northwest Frontier were inhabited by fiercely independent, well-armed Baluch and Pathan tribesmen; the dense, malarial jungles of the Northeast Frontier, by Naga and other headhunters.

Yet the very impenetrability of this barrier caused a problem for the British in India, for it meant that they, too, had little knowledge of their own borders or of the lands just beyond the frontier. Were the wily Russians turning border states hostile to British interests? And did the mountain fastness conceal hidden routes through which invading armies could threaten the Raj?

So from the north and the south, explorers and scouts sought to unravel the unknown geography, traveling as trade representatives, big-game hunters, scientists, and pilgrims. Sometimes they had military escort; sometimes they were in native disguise. Their adventures, for Russians and British alike, rivaled the legendary explorations of Henry Stanley in Africa or Hiram Bingham in South America. But the price was high. In 1842 Col. Charles Stoddart and Capt. Arthur Conolly of the Indian Army were imprisoned for months and finally beheaded by Amir Nasrullah in Bukhara. In 1869 George J. Whitaker Hayward of the Royal Geographical Society was ambushed and stabbed to death while traveling alone and in native disguise in

Yasin in the Karakoram. These two incidents were heavily publicized in the British press. Other explorers succumbed in the anonymity of secret agents to disease, altitude, punishing weather, and xenophobic natives.

In a more generalized age than our own, exploration, field sciences, intelligence, trade, and conquest were inexorably linked. The linchpin of British exploration became the Royal Engineers and Indian surveyors of the Great Trigonometrical Survey of India. At a time when Europeans had yet to climb Mont Blanc or the Matterhorn, hillmen accustomed to living at altitude and trained at a special surveying school at Dehra Dun were establishing survey stations above 20,000 feet in the Indian Himalaya.

Moreover, to cast beyond their line of sight from Indian territory, Captain Thomas George Montgomerie, Kipling's model for Colonel Creighton in *Kim*, and Major Edmund Smyth in 1866 launched one of the most dramatic and successful programs in the annals of exploration (and espionage). Noting the relative ease with which local traders and pilgrims crossed into territories forbidden to English adventurers, particularly in Tibet and Afghanistan, the two British officers began recruiting a small number of highly qualified hillmen and training them at Dehra Dun in clandestine survey techniques.

The new agents learned to count precisely measured paces, uphill and down, on modified Buddhist rosaries for hundreds of miles, to record directions with compasses concealed in walking sticks, to measure elevations by the boiling temperature of their tea water, and to record journeys sometimes lasting years on notes disguised as religious inscriptions inside prayer wheels. For three decades, this courageous and loyal band of agents, known as the Pundits (Sanskrit for "learned men"), roamed beyond the fringes of the empire with no protection but their own wits and daring, bringing the British what they needed to know and could not themselves obtain. A select few Mongolian Buddhists served the Russians in like manner.

OUR 1991 TRIP OVER THE KARAKORAM and through old Chinese Turkistan was a tantalizing glimpse of many of the legendary places of "The Great Game." Traveling by public bus, van, and eventually rail, the Wetherbees and I worked our way around the Taklimakan Desert to Turfan, eastward to Xian and Beijing, then north to Ulan Bator in Mongolia. When Harry and I reluctantly flew back to other commitments, Doris and their two teenage sons continued on to Siberia, boarded the Trans-Siberian Express to Moscow, and traveled on to western Europe. It was an interesting, educational, and occasionally adventurous trip. It was, however, 20th-century travel on established routes, akin to many similar, briefer trips they had undertaken in Pakistan, India, the former Soviet Union, and elsewhere. They were ready for something more.

"Just say what, and when." Doris's terse comment and flashing smile summed up the Wetherbees' response when I mentioned, in early 1997, my fascination with the Tsangpo gorges dating back to the mid-eighties. Initially encouraging without ever putting themselves forward as participants, they quickly became indispensable members of the organization. Their house in McLean, Virginia, was soon the expedition headquarters and Doris the reliable correspondent to answer e-mail, fax, phone, and mail. Harry applied himself to his forte, the technological end of the logistics, immersing himself in the potential communications systems (not many viable choices inside a gorge 16,000 feet deep), known historical descriptions, available maps, and satellite photography.

Cartons of freeze-dried food, foil squeeze tubes of peanut butter, and packets of crackers from military MRE rations ("John Wayne crackers") steadily filled their basement during the summer months. A mammoth stair-climbing machine, provided by the Stairmaster Corporation for conditioning drills with 50-pound backpacks, dominated the living room. It was built for a commercial gym that had many feet more headroom, and when it was running at speed the slightest variance in pace would land its occupant on the floor or cause him to hit the ceiling with his head. No Pundits were drilled more thoroughly in even pacing.

Harry's dedication to the project was whetted by his knowledge that we would be following in the footsteps, and perhaps completing the unfinished mission, of one of his 19th-century heroes: Kinthup, an illiterate Sikkimese tailor whose first exploration in Tibet ended in 1878 on the banks of the Tsangpo in Gyala. His turn-back there, perhaps from the very site where Harry set his base camp in 1998, was the preamble to a 30-year saga that spoke volumes about exploration in Tibet, duty, and the complex relationship between the British and the natives of their Indian Empire.

In 1878, Lt. (later Captain) Henry Harman, Royal Engineers, resolved to solve the puzzle of the Tsangpo-Brahmaputra linkage. He dispatched a partially trained Pundit, Nem Singh, with a menial assistant, Kinthup, from Darjeeling to the Tsangpo to follow it downstream from Tibet and see where it emerged. They got no farther than Gyala—then, as now, the end of the line before the gorge walls close in. Nevertheless, they had ventured more than 200 miles farther down the Tsangpo than any previous explorers, and while Nem Singh's survey work was considered substandard, Kinthup was recognized as a loyal and able traveler with "sturdy courage and roving propensities."[2] Still today, his stocky frame, hands folded inside the elongated sleeves of a Chinese robe, and half-hooded gaze from a surviving photograph reflect a serene and indomitable will.

Kinthup's sole, but fateful, handicap was that he was illiterate, unable to record field notes or perform the calculations required for clandestine survey. (The first and perhaps most successful Pundits were recruited from the ranks of village schoolteachers and similarly educated Indians, hence the program's Sanskrit nickname.) Accordingly. for Kinthup's next mission he was teamed up with a Mongolian lama, who was to record data while Kinthup (now code-named K.P. in Survey records) again played the role of servant.

The two were to travel as pilgrims to Gyala and attempt to progress downstream. If forced to halt, they were to cut 500 short logs, mark them with prefabricated tubes issued in Darjeeling, and throw them into the Tsangpo. Survey officers watching on the principal rivers in Assam would then be able to identify positively which one was connected to the Tsangpo. This would fall short of an actual survey, of course, but was an elegant backup plan—one, like many elaborate plans, with unintended consequences for Kinthup.

Soon after their departure from Darjeeling in the summer of 1880, the Mongolian lama began demonstrating a lack of aptitude for the life of a secret agent or for the life of a cleric. He squandered their operational funds, mistreated his "servant" Kinthup (who could not object without breaking cover), and lingered four months in the village of Thun Tsung to conduct an affair with their host's wife. By March 1881 the pair finally reached Gyala, their operational purse 25 rupees poorer after buying off the betrayed husband.

They succeeded in making their way down the right side of the river 15 miles below Gyala to a small monastery and community called Pemakochung, built about a thousand feet above the river and almost directly between the towering peaks of Namcha Barwa and Gyala Pelri. (Red Guards, or Red Guard-inspired vandals, sacked the monastery sometime during the Cultural Revolution, and the few recent visitors have reported the site deserted. From the opposite mountainside, we saw in 1998 no signs of recent occupation.)

Here the transcript of Kinthup's subsequent debriefing reported that the Tsangpo "falls over a cliff...from a height of about 150 feet." [3] That single sentence inspired speculation for the rest of the century about a massive waterfall on the Tsangpo greater than Niagara or Victoria Falls; it also led many in the Survey to disbelieve Kinthup's entire account when the falls could not be readily found. By the early 20th century two great explorers, F.M. Bailey and F. Kingdon Ward, believed they had solved the question of the waterfall. But in the final years of the century the question was to reemerge, still unresolved despite satellite imagery, aircraft, and several expeditions.

Unable to proceed farther downstream, through what is now known as the inner gorge, Kinthup and the Mongolian lama retraced their steps. They marched overland north of the great bend of the Tsangpo, intending to rejoin the river on the eastern side of the horseshoe. Twenty miles northeast of the tip of the horseshoe, the stone-walled fortress and monastery of Tongkyuk Dzong sat in a small bowl, surrounded by greening fields and white, shining mountains on every skyline like an alpine postcard.[4] Here the companions rested briefly in May 1881, until one day Kinthup learned that his ill-suited partner had departed. Worse, he had sold Kinthup to the Dzongpen (headman) as a slave. The alpine idyll was over.

For nine months Kinthup toiled as an unpaid tailor at Tongkyuk Dzong. When he finally made his bid for freedom (the long delay implies a careful premeditation rather than a headlong flight), it was, tellingly, not back along his route to safety in India, but east and down the Tsangpo, where duty lay.

Eighteen miles down the thundering tributary Po Tsangpo, traversed by a trail hung precariously on canyon walls and across rickety suspension bridges, lies the eerie, sacred site of Gompo Ne—just beyond the tributary's confluence with the main stream of the Tsangpo. Untended by monks or other inhabitants, in the lee of an island protected from the violence of the river, sheer cliff faces are lavishly decorated with sacred Buddhist inscriptions. Barked saplings by the dozens, notched with tiny steps, lean against trees and boulders to lead nats (air and water spirits) upward. Here, Kinthup rejoined the Tsangpo.[5] (Dave Phillips and I were to follow this same route almost 120 years later for the same reason: It is the natural route to the inner gorge.)

Unencumbered by freeze-dried food, Gore-Tex clothing, satellite phones, or the porters to carry them, Kinthup worked his way about 70 miles down the Tsangpo, where he was finally overtaken by his pursuers at the Marpung Monastery. Throwing himself on the mercy of the chief lama, Kinthup found himself purchased for 50 rupees, in servitude to a new master.

Ever positive, Kinthup soon made his sale a net advantage. He was again on the river, and in time his religious master became liberal in granting leave of absence for his new servant to perform pilgrimages.

Kinthup's "pilgrimages" were first to cut the 500 logs for floating down the Tsangpo to India, tie on the identifying markers with strips of bamboo, and hide the assembly in a cave until ready to launch. This he could not do until he notified the British to be watching downstream, so he eventually won permission for a longer pilgrimage of four months, ostensibly to a sacred region west of the Tsangpo's great horseshoe bend.[6] In reality he proceeded all the way to Lhasa, where he located a fellow Sikkimese willing to carry to Darjeeling a scribe-written letter, part of which raises a question about where the British might have learned their art of laconic understatement.

With the letter dispatched and nothing but familiar and relatively safe routes between himself and home, Kinthup retraced, alone, the dangerous route back to remote eastern Tibet and voluntary slavery to be in position to release the logs the following November as promised. At least temporarily, his luck changed: The Lama of Marpung Monastery was so impressed by his return and his zeal for pilgrimages that he granted Kinthup his freedom. Kinthup remained at Marpung making money for his long return journey, and over the appointed three days in November 1883 he released the logs. Then, incredibly, he departed not back along the routes he knew so well toward home, but farther downriver into unknown, certainly hostile, and possible headhunter tribal areas.

The primitive and xenophobic tribes of the Assam jungle proved too much even for the indomitable Kinthup (they were for the British Army as well), and he eventually was forced to retrace his steps back through Tibet. When he finally strode up the steep cobbled alleys of Darjeeling, a full four years after his dispatch, he had floated the logs down the Tsangpo as ordered by then Lieutenant Harman and walked to within 40 miles of British-controlled territory on the Brahmaputra, missing only the 10-mile segment within the inner gorge. If ever a returning explorer deserved a hero's welcome, it was Kinthup.

Neither the fates nor the bureaucrats were through with Kinthup yet, however. Captain Harman lay dead in Europe, victim of disease and severe exposure from surveying in the fetid jungles and extreme elevations of India's Northeast Frontier. Kinthup's letter had fallen into a bureaucratic black hole; the logs prepared and launched down the Tsangpo at such great cost to Kinthup had floated unremarked past British outposts on the Brahmaputra that were completely unaware of the late Captain Harman's plan or Kinthup's schedule.

Worse, a new generation of Survey officers found Kinthup's tale incredible and scorned his reporting for its lack of written documentation. "Sturdy courage" and the near-photographic memory typical of many illiterates were no match for a class prejudice against the stocky, uneducated tailor from the hills of Sikkim. For the next 30 years, the Raj's loyal agent was to toil in menial capacities in the hill stations of the empire, plying his trade as a tailor between occasional engagements with expeditions into the mountains.[7]

THE ERA OF CLANDESTINE EXPLORATION OF TIBET by the Pundits ended abruptly in 1899. Col. Sir Francis Younghusband reintroduced the tradition of travel and exploration by the British themselves, at the head of a 2,000-man invasion force supported by more than 10,000 porters and an equal number of mules, bullocks, yaks, and ponies, investing Lhasa. Kinthup was there, representing the old order as a humble assistant to Captain Waddell of the Indian Medical Service. There, too, was a young officer who was to become a leader in the next generation of explorers in the Tsangpo gorges. There is no indication that Kinthup and Lt. F.M. Bailey, Indian Political Service, ever met during the Lhasa campaign, but their lives were to become linked by the mighty river, leading to a dramatic meeting in Simla almost two decades later.

Bailey's fascination with, and preparation for, exploration of the gorges grew while on other explorations of western Tibet for Younghusband, during a tour as British Agent in the Tibetan city of Gyangze, and on two unsuccessful attempts to reach the gorges themselves. By 1913 he was fluent in Tibetan, experienced in travel across Asia, and determined to be the first to follow the Tsangpo from Tibet to British India. When his chance came, he accomplished the reverse. Wangling assignment to a military task force surveying its way up the river from Assam, he managed to contact ethnic Tibetans living well south of the usual line between Tibet and Assam. When they agreed to show him their tenuous route back to their homeland, Bailey recruited Captain Moorfield of the Royal Engineers as companion, surveyor, and co-conspirator. Stretching their orders to the breaking point and uncertain whether they would be met upon return with accolades or reprimands, the two split from the main body and disappeared northward into Tibet.

Over the course of several months, through every kind of physical and political difficulty, Bailey and Moorfield worked their way up the river. They did not, in the end, cover as much of the river's course as had Kinthup; politics required them to detour to the regional capital to obtain permission to travel onward. These, however, were two British officers keeping detailed journals. Moorfield was even making a plane-table map from every vantage point. There would be no questioning of their reports. The Royal Geographical Society would bestow medals, not scorn.

Yet with every step, Bailey realized more and more the veracity of the report Kinthup had dictated 30 years previously, archived without remark in the Survey's voluminous files. Place names and descriptions left no doubt that Kinthup had traveled as he said he had, and the discrepancies in times and distances could be expected from anyone fleeing slavery. There was one glaring exception, however. When Bailey and Moorfield finally worked their way north of the great loop, through Tongkyuk Dzong and around from Gyala to Pemakochung, they found no sign of a 150-foot waterfall on the Tsangpo. The two British officers explored a few miles downstream but were soon forced to halt by dangerous cliffs and deceitful Monpa guides.[8] The single most dramatic geographic feature Kinthup had reported was not to be found.

Kinthup's tale preyed on Bailey as he marched across Tibet and Bhutan, back to British India: the remarkable adventure and determination to complete the mission, the scorned report that proved so accurate, the waterfall that aroused such interest but seemed not to exist. Bailey resolved to track down the Pundit, if he still lived, and learn the facts firsthand.

Bailey persevered and finally had Kinthup traced to his tailor shop in the alleyways of Darjeeling and brought to Simla for a revealing interview. By then in his 60s, Kinthup told Bailey he clearly recalled reporting a 20- or 30-foot waterfall on the Tsangpo near Pemakochung, and a 150-foot waterfall, with sacred images behind the curtain of water, on a small side stream across the river from Gyala. Bailey could only conclude that the translator confused the two as a single waterfall; Kinthup's vindication was complete.

Then, in a gesture as honorable as Kinthup's first reception home was shameful, Captain Bailey made it his mission to confront the bureaucrats, redeem Kinthup officially, and obtain for him a pension or stipend for his loyal service. Within months of receiving a thousand rupees in belated recognition of his achievements, the old explorer died. Perhaps after 30 years his sturdy courage and endurance had finally led him over his last and most difficult mountain.

JAMIE'S SHIFTS OF FORTUNE WERE NOT NEARLY AS DRAMATIC as slavery, escape, and pursuit. Nor did he have to walk all the way to Lhasa to send letters overland to home. When he awoke the next morning at Harry's base camp in Gyala, over the satellite telephone Jamie caught up with family business: Eldest daughter Katelin, 19, was off balance away from home as a college freshman in New York, and youngest Darcy, 8, was off balance with Daddy away from home on expedition.

Although his brother Tom lives months of each year on the road with his kayaking school (typically Mexico in the winter, West Virginia in the spring, Colorado in the summer, Canada in the fall), Jamie's family is not fond of extended separations.

When Jamie determined that training for the 1992 Barcelona Olympics would best be accomplished near the competition site, the family relocated for a year to a home in the French Pyrenees. Transferring four youngsters to French schools while his wife Sandra managed her extensive business as a cartoonist by long distance across the Atlantic might not be many athletes' ideal training environment, but Jamie's priorities lay in the heart of this turbulent dynamic family.

The satellite telephone was not just a convenience linking us to home. Our modern effort to travel light and fast, particularly on the river, made the expedition very dependent upon foolproof support and resupply, and thus on communications between the elements. Although small walkie-talkie radios were useful between paddlers on opposite sides of the river, the walls of the gorge blocked all but the shortest transmissions—except upward. Harry Wetherbee devoted the best part of two years testing various communications systems and, more difficult, coordinating with Chinese officials in Beijing to lease officially licensed satellite phones.[9] The bureaucracy was numbing and the e-mail interminable, but at the last moment Harry accomplished the miraculous and had three working Inmarsat Mini-M's delivered in Lhasa—one for each element of the expedition.

At five-and-a-half pounds each, with packaging and batteries extra, these invaluable devices were just on the border of practical for the boating team. Batteries were the severely limiting factor because of their weight and because they would drain, slowly but unpredictably over time. Each support team carried a solar-panel recharger, but these were of limited utility in the cloud forest, with the team on the march during most daylight hours. Thus, except when traveling with the trucks or in a base camp, phone usage was severely limited. Routine reports were standardized and exchanged in less than a minute, every second day, unless events dictated otherwise.

Satellite communications were not the only technological rabbit Harry pulled from his hat, allowing us to throw ourselves into the gorges with a measure of confidence not enjoyed by previous explorers. Two days prior to our departure from the United States, a courier from Federal Express picked his way across the welter of equipment, food packages, and canvas duffels strewn about the Wetherbees' lawn in McLean, Virginia, to deliver a long cardboard tube from Colorado. It contained computer-enhanced satellite photographs of our expedition route, a first-ever look at areas never seen by surveyors or Western explorers and not portrayed accurately on topographic maps.[10] With GPS (Global Positioning System) in hand, it was hard to believe we were only a century removed from Kinthup, counting his paces on a rosary.

NO TECHNOLOGY MAKES THE SLIGHTEST DIFFERENCE to the hard reality of rock, ice, thin air, and raging water, nor to the mystical significance assigned to every feature of this colossal landscape. It was plain, old-fashioned karma that appeared the following morning in the guise of two figures slowly picking their way up the far side of the river and riding the ferry across to base camp. Team members were later to disagree on whether these were pilgrims or hunters. With the unusually carnivorous form of Buddhism frequently practiced in the Pemako region, the distinction sometimes seemed to rest on whether the seekers had found anything to shoot yet. Through Pemba Sherpa's halting translation, it emerged that the pair had found Jamie's boat floating in a huge eddy on the left side of the river a mile or two downstream. They had dragged it safely ashore, and they could produce it on demand. Armed pilgrimage was thirsty work, however, and a minimum of 2,000 yuan ($250.00) would be required for their services.

With his miraculously revived hopes and dreams dependent upon recovering the boat, Jamie would likely have paid ten times that sum. But 2,000 yuan was probably more than the entire annual cash income of the village of Gyala. The inflationary pressures of such an injection of funds were incalculable, not to mention the effect on future prices of all goods and services to foreigners. Besides, negotiations were a communal activity, the local spectator sport, the only substitute for theater and film and television. Jamie's capitulation to this demand would have had the same effect as an eagerly anticipated heavyweight championship fight ending in a KO in the first round.

Jamie played his role. Still through Pemba Sherpa's painstaking translation—local dialect to Tibetan to Nepali to English—with Harry his executive agent and Paulo as technical advisor, he confronted the pilgrims, while the piratical ferryman and the entire population of Gyala served as chorus. Harry's first counteroffer of 500 yuan was met with stony contempt. Paulo reminded everyone that vast and unseen powers had great interest in the outcome of our enterprise: Officials in faraway Lhasa had issued permits; from even farther away the unfathomable NGS and NPR waited for reports. No one in Gyala should want to be perceived obstructive.

In Tibet, of course, vast and unseen powers lurk in every spring and stone, and they are expected to manifest themselves periodically if they desire to be taken seriously. By the third and final act an hour and a half later, Harry therefore conceded that he would consult with higher authority. With the external speaker set at its loudest, he dialed the satellite telephone with many chirps and tones, then held a long and animated conversation in English about friends and family with his father in Chapel Hill, North Carolina. Returning to the negotiating table, he reported that his elders recommended compromising on 800 yuan. This was deemed acceptable if Jamie would also throw in a nylon tarpaulin, and the deal was done. The crowds spilled out of the theater, happily exclaiming over their colleagues' unbelievable windfall, as Jamie and Pemba made arrangements with their new best friends to recover the boat the following day.

The tumultuous day ended with the arrival of Tom, Doug, and Roger, stroking side by side down the wide, swift river into camp. For them it had been a diamond day, one of those rare, clear days that etch themselves in memory and draw travelers back to the Himalaya like an addictive drug. The icy summit of Namcha Barwa reflected bright sunlight impossibly high over their heads, still far enough away to be appreciated as a vast but singular mountain. Deeper in the gorge its massive flanks would block views of the summit, with only hints of massive ice fields appearing like gleaming UFOs in rents in the clouds. Around bend after bend the big rapids had offered the paddlers clean lines through. Huge holes appeared periodically to their left and right, pounding reminders of the penalties if they were to miscalculate the route, and Tom noted soberly how difficult it was to appreciate their size and power from above. But throughout the long day the lines opened up and the rapids were run, and the three arrived at the ferry landing in Gyala elated and encouraged.

THE FOLLOWING DAY THE UNITED SUPPORT AND RIVER TEAMS completed the warm-up phase of the trip at the "Video Rapid," a long complex of big waves and huge holes readily accessible by trail just downstream from Gyala. In tribute to both karma and modern plastics technology, Jamie's boat had been recovered completely undamaged after washing through miles of river that had taken the paddlers two days to navigate, with several carries. Even the waterproof bags of gear within were intact. One final day to shake down equipment and for Jamie to get back in the groove would also be videographer Paulo Castillo's last, and best, opportunity to video the team on the water. Henceforth, except for brief encounters with the support teams for resupply, filming, both video and still, would be limited to what the team members themselves could accomplish.

From the earliest planning stages it was clear there would be severe restraints on the equipment the paddlers could carry and on the attention they could give to photography under increasingly arduous conditions. Yet recording the expedition was important: We had a responsibility to the sport and to future expeditions to report our experience and lessons learned. It was also a vital interest of our primary sponsor—the National Geographic Society—and an obligation to the host of equipment sponsors. Tom McEwan carried a palm-size digital video camera, his brother had a professional SLR, and both Doug and Roger carried waterproof point-and-shoot cameras readily available on their life jackets. This would ensure basic coverage throughout.

To add an extra measure of thoroughness and profession-alism, every effort was made to obtain good photography dur-ing this first phase of the river journey. The river team was practicing anyway on less stressful water, trails paralleled the river for access from shore, and the Wetherbee support team was on hand to carry in and out the extra camera gear and exposed film. Whatever transpired during the progressively less predictable later stages of the expedition, some useful material would be "in the can." Paulo would shoot everything he could of the expedition while accompanying the support elements, of course, but it was primarily the plan for these reliable sev-eral days beside the paddlers that made it worthwhile for National Geographic Television to attach him to the expedition at the last minute.

With long black hair and a flashing white smile in a per-petually tanned countenance, Paulo was clad except in cold-est weather in nylon river shorts and Teva sandals; he was younger than the tight-knit group of old friends on the expe-dition. His easy humor, quiet competence while traveling, and professional approach to filming quickly fit him into the team, however. When not behind the camera, Paulo guides white-water rafting trips around the world, from China's Yangtze River to Chile's Bio-Bio, so he was no stranger to what we were attempting. Doubtless he arrived chafing at his restriction to the support element and intending somehow to travel at least part of the route on the water—any of us would have felt the same way. When that was not to be, however, he gracefully fit in where he could, filming every aspect of the expedition within his range and contributing everything he could to the team effort.

Before leaving Washington, Tom had taken his new, blue-and-red expedition kayak to the fabricating shop in the basement of the National Geographic Society headquarters. There the inventive crew installed lightweight attachments near the bow and stern for a removable pedestal holding a waterproof camera housing. The cumbersome camera and housing suspended a foot above the end of the boat would interfere far too much with maneuvering and Eskimo-rolling for regular use, and the weight and bulk could only be carried by the support crew. Now, however, was the occasion they had planned for: The rapid was straightforward, a pool below offered room for rescue if problems arose, and Paulo and the support crew were at hand.

Six to eight times each, the paddlers ran the rapid and carried again to the top. Paulo positioned his tripod-mounted video camera with telephoto lens in a variety of viewpoints throughout the day. And with both still and video cameras mounted on the ends of his boat, Tom made multiple runs to get the "up close and personal" perspectives.

In testing the system before departure, on the Great Falls of the Potomac outside Washington, D.C., it had been easy to trigger the camera from shore with a handheld remote control device. But on the vastly bigger Tsangpo, it quickly became apparent that the radio signal was too short-range to work as planned. Not one to accept insubordination from technology, Doug Gordon fixed the remote transmitter to the middle of his paddle shaft with duct tape and chased Tom down the center of the Class V rapid, triggering the camera from a distance of 50 to 100 feet.

The only shortfall in photographic coverage lay in still

photography. Jamie's SLR camera system was the sole casualty of his swim, and his backup had already been dispatched to the first resupply point downstream in the incorrect anticipation that it would not be needed earlier. After the photo session at the Video Rapid, he filled the gap with the Nikon that had been sent specifically for the mount on Tom's boat, but that was equipped only with a wide-angle lens (as were the point-and-shoot cameras carried by Doug and Roger). This could not possibly reach out and capture the drama and action of kayaking on the huge river as would a telephoto, and in the end the video portrayal of the river was notably more dramatic than the stills.

Later that afternoon, back upstream at the Gyala base camp, Jamie compulsively packed and repacked each item of equipment, agonizing one last time over choices of climbing gear, reconsidering every ounce. Doug studied the satellite imagery yet again in minutest detail, analyzing the elevation data and its implications about where the greatest difficulties would lie. Tom and Roger, with the assistance of Harry, Doris, and Pemba Sherpa, redivided food supplies, for the team had decided to proceed downstream with a 15-day supply in their boats, rather than the nine originally planned.

After their firsthand taste of conditions, the paddlers no longer thought of traveling through the entire gorge. Perhaps that had been wishful thinking from the beginning; certainly with the extra difficulties of the flooded river it was not to be. Still practical, however, was exploring downstream to rendezvous with Dave Phillips and me at the first resupply point just upstream from Rainbow Falls, roughly 28 miles by river from Gyala.

Several previous travelers had made it on foot that far (but no farther) down the right side of the river, although not directly on the river all the way: F. Kingdon Ward and Lord Cawdor in 1924, and more recently Jill Bielawski, Ken Storm, Ian Baker, and Eric Manthey in 1994. The left bank, from which Dave and I would be approaching, was, as far as we knew, never explored, and we hoped it might offer a route into the completely unknown section of the inner gorge below Rainbow Falls.

After more than an hour of animated group deliberation the four decided to continue with the boats, expecting at some point to abandon them and proceed entirely on foot. Every hundred yards they could gain on the water saved time and backbreaking effort. Moreover, even with the high water the option to cross occasionally from bank to bank was an invaluable tool, one unavailable to previous explorers. Doug dubbed this approach "boat-assisted hiking."

CHAPTER 5

ALPINE STYLE

...austere and perilous journeys, pursued in seclusion [achieve]
between the adventurer and his surroundings
an always heightened sense of the humour,
the beauty and the deeper, harder values of a life
lived under natural conditions.

—GEOFFREY WINTHROP YOUNG

RUNNING THROUGH the "Video Rapid" and on downstream on the morning of October 11, Tom McEwan noted with satisfaction that the rapid differed noticeably from the previous day's photographic exercise: The water level had dropped overnight.

Harry, Doris, Paulo, and Pemba were falling steadily behind, packing gear at Gyala for their return trek to the vehicles at Pei; Dave and I were high in the mountains downstream, heading on foot for the resupply point near Rainbow Falls. From this point on, with each passing day Tom expected a sense of freedom, simplicity, and center to build for the four paddlers. Forced to focus all daily thoughts on the physical task at hand, their only nightly concerns would be the primitive requirements of food, shelter, and recuperation from the day's exertion. An intense sense of teamwork would develop, their long friendships and previous river experiences evolving with the isolation and mutual danger into a tribal, almost telepathic cohesion.

Their further challenge, likely the difference between success and failure, lay in finding a way of going, of moving with a kind of rhythm through this majestic landscape and working as a team that somehow included not only the four humans but also the water and rocks and vegetation—even the air. All of white-water sport involves being at one with the power of flowing water; here, in the depths of a canyon unmatched on the planet, they knew they must factor in the entire surrounding landscape. Whether they named it Dorje Phagmo (the Diamond Sow) or dioritic gneiss probably did not matter.

The dun-colored, semiarid hillsides of the Tibetan Plateau had now steepened and responded to the leading edge of moist air sucked up the canyon from the Bay of Bengal. In every direction the flanks of Gyala Pelri and Namcha Barwa rose like vast green thunderheads, punctuated by gray curtains of cliff and the occasional rock-encrusted snout of a descending glacier. Between the encircling walls the roar of the water was unceasing, a hindrance to conversation and a reminder of the colossal river, day and night.

Progress was steady at first. Paddling was virtually impossible in the powerful main stream of current, and places to safely cross from one bank to the other were rare. The still high water level linked together rapids that would later be separated by pools. The group cautiously picked their way down the left shore, though, and satisfying mileage fell behind them.

By noon the shoreline became steeper, and the river funneled into an unrunnable rapid. We saw huge holes followed by a train of mammoth waves, flanked on either side by eddies, feeding down to where the rocketing current slammed into a cliff along the left-hand shore several hundred yards below. In this treacherous zone of sheer rock and impacting water, explosion waves shot geysers of spume 20 feet into the air. From a safe crossing spot above, the paddlers split into pairs and began to scout on foot for the way around this monster.

DOWN THE LEFT SIDE, CLOSE FRIENDS DOUG AND JAMIE worked along the steepening bank. They needed hardly a word to synchronize their movements after two recent expeditions in British Columbia, years of paddling and traveling together on the international slalom racing circuit, and thousands of hours encouraging each other to push their limits in the series of training gates they had hung on the Housatonic River near Jamie's old Connecticut farmhouse. On the water their judgments and conclusions almost always coincided without discussion, and in making bivouac camps they shared tasks with swift, long-practiced efficiency.

"You know, one thing that makes all this portaging and hiking worthwhile is the great smell of these herbs." Doug Gordon's comment stopped Jamie in his tracks. The two had been scouting for hours, sweat pouring from their faces. The tops of their dry suits were rolled down and tied off at their waists, and their hands stung from accidentally grasping nettles in their search for balance along the steep dirt-and-gravel bank. Suddenly Jamie became aware of a rich and pungent smell that had surrounded them all day, given off by low bushes they clung to for security.

"Doug was probably the most rational of all of us," Tom observed. "Rational" was a word often used to describe Doug. His flashing grin and obvious delight could stem equally from discovering an unknown chemical process visible only by electron microscope or from nailing the clean, smooth line down the center of a huge rapid, helping a beginning kayaker accomplish his first Eskimo roll, or simply experiencing his surroundings more fully than most people ever do.

"Now the averages are irrelevant; now it's the absolutes that count," Doug sometimes commented as he put on his spray skirt. Perhaps the challenge of finding order in the chaos of white water, of following reasoning with physical results for high stakes, is particularly attractive to the scientific mind. Since the earliest days of the sport, a disproportionate number of scientists and engineers have been in the forefront of white-water sport, and Doug exemplified this fraternity.[2]

HE LEARNED TO KAYAK WHILE RUNNING THE BIG, STEEP RIVERS of Washington, Oregon, and California in the 1970s, but by the early-1970s intellectual challenges led him to the Department of Chemistry at Harvard and reduced his daily paddling to the flat Charles River. Quick to identify and embrace the greatest available challenges, whatever the field, Doug resolved to polish his kayaking skills through slalom racing. At least temporarily, he exchanged the high-volume wilderness rivers of the West for the small, steep rivers and tricky man-made white-water racecourses of the East Coast and Europe. He learned to place his boat not just on the clean line down a rapid but within inches of slalom poles, contesting for fractions of seconds in speed against many of the world's strongest paddlers. The U.S. Team coaches, established racers, and young, aggressive contenders in the slalom world soon learned that this older college graduate and emerging scientist "not only worked harder than anyone else, he worked smarter than anyone else."[3]

There followed a decade of balancing elite slalom racing with industrial research chemistry, seasons of World Cup and World Championships competition intermingled with publication of articles like "Gas-Phase Pyrolysis of tert-Butyl-(ally)selenium, a New Precursor for Organometalic Chemical Vapor Deposition of ZnSe" in peer review journals. He had medals and patents. When Doug retired from the U.S. Team after the 1987 World Championships and returned to his first love of running rivers, he did so with an undiminished zest for exploration and discovery, and with mind and body trained to exacting standards.

ROGER AND TOM FOLLOWED A PARALLEL COURSE down the opposite bank. Though not as close as "the slalom team" across the river, Tom and Roger shared many years of association on Appalachian rivers, particularly on Roger's home river, the upper Youghiogheny of western Maryland where Roger based his white-water rafting business. They also shared a long rivalry and mutual respect that grew out of wildwater racing, an event analogous to downhill skiing, timed from point to point downriver for speed alone, without gates or other embellishments. Jamie and Roger had briefly been teammates when both represented the U.S. at the Wildwater World Championships in 1988, but Roger's pairing with Tom to form "the wildwater team" flowed naturally both from their long association and their converging approach to the Tsangpo.

As had happened before, the two brothers, seeking to share experiences through the bright prism of expedition life, did not find a natural partnership. Like two strong magnets of identical polarity, they seemed to approach only so close and no closer.

ACROSS THE WIDE RIVER THE TWO TEAMS CONFERRED about their options over palm-size walkie-talkies. Jamie and Doug found the cliffs becoming steeper and more difficult, while Tom and Roger confidently concluded that after a short but difficult carry around the head of the big rapid, they could reenter the river and run down along the right shore. When "the slalom team" returned to their boats and paddled across the Tsangpo, the reunited foursome began the arduous carry, taking turns cutting trail through thick undergrowth with the half-size machete Tom carried inside his boat.

Emerging at last beside the huge wave train in midstream, they launched with relief into the water and began to paddle cautiously downstream. Even running conservative routes next to (sneaking down) the shoreline was thrilling; the drops were not very difficult, but all knew they could not afford the slightest miscalculation, because the rapids below were monstrous. From their experience in the very first rapid back at Pei, from Jamie's nearly expedition-ending swim, and from less dramatic but nevertheless important daily reminders like unexpected flips and Eskimo rolls in the turbulent eddies, the Tsangpo had taught them that several of the safety and rescue systems they could rely upon on other, smaller rivers were simply not available. No teammate could paddle blindly downstream to drag to shore a swimmer or lost equipment, and the 70-foot throw ropes they all carried on shore could reach only a tiny percentage of the several-hundred-foot-wide river.

Each paddler's safety was almost exclusively in his own hands—in his judgment, in his boat control, and in his unfailing Eskimo roll when capsized. The roll, where the paddler rights his overturned boat with a snap of his hips and a simultaneous twist of the paddle for purchase, is every paddler's first line of defense; but, it is useless if the boat is trapped, either in a big ricirculating hole or pinned against rocks. And, as with everything else on the Tsangpo, the maneuver was considerably more difficult with the loaded expedition boats and in the unceasing turbulence even in the eddy water. To achieve more surety, they scaled back the levels of difficulty that they attempted.

All priority lay in never allowing themselves to run downstream into a trap, where they could neither continue nor retreat. Maj. John Wesley Powell summed up this ultimate river-runner's nightmare in his diary of the first descent of the Grand Canyon of the Colorado in 1867:

> *May be we shall come to a fall in these canyons which we cannot pass, where the walls rise from the water's edge so that we cannot land, and where the water is so swift that we cannot return…. How will it be in the future?*[4]

A kayak can sprint into any eddy or halt like a salmon behind virtually any rock. Such ability generally provides much greater flexibility on unknown rivers than that provided by either the sizable oak dories used by Major Powell or the modern rafts that are so useful in carrying supplies and unskilled passengers once a safe route is known. The small, torpedo-shaped, and very durable boat's greater portability on shore, too, adds up to a tool uniquely suited to exploration.

On the Tsangpo, the four paddlers' equipment, skills, judgment, and endurance were facing an unprecedented test. As evening approached, even paddling along the shoreline became too difficult. Jamie led the climb up a small cliff, from which vantage point they could see their way down the right bank blocked by a broken cliff. Surmounting that obstacle would require a climb of about 1,200 feet. Across the river lay a much more promising route.

THE FOUR TIRED AND DISHEARTENED PADDLERS rappelled down to their boats, leaned into the unwelcome task of carrying all their gear back upstream to the safe crossing place, and made camp at the first opportunity. Roger had by now become team quartermaster by unspoken agreement, examining the shoreline and making campsite decisions following a routine that had evolved on previous trips. Beginning an hour and a half before sunset, they would stop at any ideal campsite; such gifts are not to be disdained. An hour before sunset, they would halt at any adequate spot; a half hour later, any place would do where patches of sand between the boulders offered space for four men to lie down. Aside from enough daylight to gather firewood, their requirements were rudimentary.

What the packing crate is to the man with no home, the bivouac sack has traditionally been to the camper with no tent. A protective sausage skin fitting over the sleeping bag, it was developed to save the lives of mountain climbers stranded away from their camps. It features no extra space for gear, dressing, or cooking, and for years the available "waterproof" fabrics were always more efficient at condensing the body's own vapor into icy puddles inside than in keeping rain and snow out. Until recently, the bivouac sack, or "bivvy," was never the habitation of choice; it was only of dire necessity.

The advent of fabrics that are not only waterproof but also breathable has transformed the humble bivvy. Each paddler's "castle" fits in the palm of a hand and is an ultralight, sophisticated combination of rugged, waterproof floor, vapor-porous Gore-Tex, top, fiberglass poles, and weatherproof zips and seals. When used with lightweight sleeping bags and thin sleeping pads for insulation and padding, these shelters proved more than adequate under almost all conditions. They had the virtue of fitting into the terrain where even small tents could not be pitched, and to the exhausted paddlers they were four small cocoons of warmth and privacy in which to rejuvenate each night.

Once cozied into a modern bivvy, a person is wonderfully weatherproof, but undressing and entering its confines without flooding in a pouring rain remains nearly impossible. A lightweight, eight-by-ten-foot nylon tarpaulin was shared by the four campers and could be hung in various configurations to protect a bivvy entrance or a cooking area, for example.

An axiom of Tom's was that given adequate food and a good night's rest, they could endure almost any amount of stress during the day. Throughout the preceding summer, Doris and Harry had painstakingly assembled food supplies that. like their shelter, were a combination of lightweight simplicity and modern technology. The team carried a small gas stove for emergencies, but an open fire of driftwood usually provided warmth, comfort, and boiling water from a shared titanium pot, their only cooking requirement. Breakfasts were instant hot cereal, tea, coffee, or cocoa, and cold lunches were trail mix, crackers with cheese spread and peanut butter, and high-energy Clif Bars. Dinners primarily consisted of commercially packaged freeze-dried meals that were eaten directly out of their packages with the single spoon each man carried.

Working athletes can require three or more times the calories of the average person (4,000 to 6.000 calories daily are not unusual at Olympic training tables), so the weight and bulk of food, even dried, were the most significant variables in loads for both boats and porters. Furthermore, unlike on our normal river trips or in a single competition, our stress levels and special diet needs would last almost two months. With weight, nutrition, and palatability all critical, Doris added an extra level of specialization.

After surveying each member of the expedition about dietary preferences and caloric requirements, experiences on previous expeditions, favored specific entrees from the major manufacturers, secret trail mix formulas, and daily multivitamins and other supplements, she assembled meal packs for each individual. Jamie was unchallenged as "team gourmet," shipping cases of dried fruits, nuts, cereals, protein powder, unsweetened chocolate, and special-formula energy bars to Doris for inclusion. Each daily ration was assembled and vacuum sealed in plastic, which protected it not only from premature rehydration in the wet boats and damp climate but also from pilfering of delectables by porters during transport.

Stomachs pacified by a hot bulky meal and minds lulled by the universal hypnotism of the open fire, the four finished each long day with mugs of hot cocoa, a brief review of the day, and plans for the morrow. Conversation was difficult, however,

over the din of the river, and they seldom lingered later than
nine o'clock before separating to their bivvies.

IN OUR PARLANCE, OUR PADDLING WAS NOW "ALPINE STYLE"—a term
we had unabashedly adopted from the climbing world. The
chairman of the Royal Geographical Society who, beginning in
1919, planned and organized the first several British attempts
to climb Everest was, significantly, Sir Francis Younghusband.
This man, who had led both Kinthup and F.M. Bailey to Lhasa
along with 2,000 troops, did so with a logistics train of 10,091
porters, 7,096 mules, 5,234 bullocks, 2,668 ponies, 4,465 yaks,
and 6 (lonely) camels. The commander's personal gear included
67 shirts, a full dress coat, a morning coat, two jaeger coats, a
shikar hat, a khaki helmet, a white panama hat, a thin solar
topi, and so on, filling 29 containers.[5] With this Edwardian
excess the model, small wonder the first years of Everest climbing were characterized by armies of porters, base camps resembling small cities, military zeal, and nationalistic jingoism.

By the 1930s a counterculture began to emerge, pioneered
by H.W. Tilman and Eric Shipton, who disparaged the former
approach as "siege tactics." In contrast, they demonstrated the
utility of an alpine style, climbing with smaller, self-contained
parties as mountaineering had evolved in the Swiss Alps. They
still used a limited number of porters, shuttled supplies forward
when necessary, and climbed by establishing a series of high-
altitude camps above a fixed base. But their "tooth-to-tail ratio"
was radically different. These pukka sahibs carried as much or
more than any porter and lived as frugally, and over the course
of several expeditions in the Himalaya and the Karakoram,
Tilman and Shipton proved they could travel quickly and lightly

through a landscape their predecessors had treated as alien and hostile territory. More recently, a few transcendent climbers, such as Reinhold Messner, have carried this approach to its logical conclusion with unsupported solo assents of Mount Everest and other major summits.

In our white-water analogy, "alpine style" meant running rivers with all requirements inside the white-water boats, independent of supplies carried by accompanying rafts or from camps positioned in advance. Doug described one special morning in British Columbia:

> *The plateau was rocky and there were barely enough level spots for our three bivvy sacs—but the steep terrain and poor access to the river also lessened the chances that an inquisitive grizzly would bother us.... After retrieving our food bags from where they hung suspended in mid-air by our throw ropes, I made myself a large cup of coffee and clambered down to the river to watch the sun rise over the canyon walls. Mornings like this make self-supported expeditions my favorite form of paddling. There were no boats to load, no shuttle to run, no cars, no real evidence at all of civilization other than the few brightly colored scraps of nylon, fiberglass, and polyethylene we had brought with us. I sat alone with my thoughts in a spot which had been visited by few humans and left almost no trace of my presence.*[6]

Tom, Jamie, and I had planned and equipped our expedition in Bhutan to travel this way, but in the end our Bhutanese hosts proved unwilling to have us out of sight of their escorts for longer than a day at a time. We had to run predetermined river segments to camps established nightly by the Bhutanese support crew, severely limiting the exploration we could accomplish. We (particularly Tom) vowed that next time would be different.

Over the next 15 years, we experimented in Mexico and Canada with progressively longer and more difficult self-contained descents, building confidence and refining equipment. Doug, already a friend of Jamie's from the U.S. Slalom Team, first joined this experiment in 1986, spending six days with me between the soaring, 2,000-foot limestone walls of Mexico's Moctezuma Canyon.

Three years later he first paddled with Tom on Quebec's Aguanus River, ten days of unbroken wilderness and big white water. Each recognized in the other a kindred spirit: They shared a joy in the physical and mental challenge of the water, measuring their skill and judgment against always changing and unforgiving standards. Doug wrote of one spot halfway down the Aguanus:

>...the river had grown to 20 times its original volume. The power of 15,000 cubic feet per second falling over 20-foot drops was both inspiring and intimidating.... Marked on the map as a 25-foot falls, it was a hundred-yard arc of falling water broken two-thirds of the way down by a smooth, green, angled ramp. The falls ended in the inevitable explosion of white foam. There was a hint of recirculation on the left side, but the main flow went to the right of it. And no mistake about it, where the water went was where I would end up. For all my years of racing, for all the hundreds of hours I had spent putting my boat within inches of slalom poles

in difficult rapids, in water like this I would relinquish control to the river as soon as I crossed the lip of the falls. The key therefore was to come over the lip in the right spot. Luckily there was an ideal landmark. A tiny green curl of water on the left side of the ramp would make it easy to gauge my position as I approached.

...Mike was in his boat below the falls, ready to pick up the pieces if necessary. I was disconcerted to see how small Mike looked, bobbing in the waves below, and I was dismayed to realize that my tiny landmark curler on the lip towered at least five feet over my head. It was too late to worry. I felt my boat accelerate suddenly and braced for the impact in the cauldron below. It never came. With a shower of white, like falling while skiing in three feet of fresh powder, I emerged unscathed beside Mike. Even if we had walked everything from here to the Gulf of St. Lawrence, the trip would have been a success.[7]

TO A DEGREE THAT SET THEM APART FROM MOST of their fellow paddlers, both Tom and Doug delighted in making their own judgments and setting their own standards, independent of peer support or validation. Without sacrificing safety or support for the group, almost from the beginning the two paddled somewhat apart, on a different plane from the rest of us on that trip. They paddled rapids, in one case a whole canyon, which we did not. The two frequently ran different routes, comparing notes and reasons afterward; they chased each other joyfully down a river I found arduous.

That independence of mind has led on occasion to Tom's

being labeled an extremist by people who think he defies the conventional wisdom in our sport; they do not realize he sets standards for himself alone and not for others to follow. In Doug, he saw a companion who would not blindly follow his example, who would proceed on his own individual choice and confidence. This distinction becomes all important when sport reaches the level where death can result from miscalculations, and phrases such as "sure, you can do it" or "follow me" can have tragic consequences. The burden for the leader can be greater than for the follower.

Exercising freedom of choice and taking joy from trusting one's own judgment has a negative pole, of course. Near the end of the Aguanus River, in a final paroxysm before merging into the tidal reaches of the lower St. Lawrence, the entire river plunges at fire-hose velocity for a quarter mile through the Saw Cut, a 40-foot wide cleft in the tortured Precambrian metamorphics of the Canadian Shield. No kayaker could survive that power; none would consider trying. Just upstream on the river's left is a small eddy with an easy take-out for the carryaround, its approach guarded by a large recirculating hole with only a narrow line to skirt its edge. Here Tom elected to run his boat down to the eddy, while Doug walked down to watch from a rocky vantage point—throw rope in hand, as always when scouting.

Although Tom had been paddling his laden boat continuously for nine days and it was lighter than its starting weight by that amount of food, this time the weight of the gear unaccountably made him miss his chosen line. He plunged into the hole; the boat rapidly cartwheeled several times end-over-end, then fell sideways, pinned against the white wall of recirculating water.

Trapped in the maelstrom, Tom elected to swim out. This was not an easy choice to make, because he doubted he could avoid being swept into the Saw Cut, and he thought he would almost certainly wash out of the hole beyond the range of Doug's rope. Tom was absolutely certain, however, that he would be unable to save himself if he remained trapped in the hole until his reserves of oxygen were expended.

Readying himself for a smooth and rapid exit into water flowing beneath the hole and away from the boat—which would quickly take on water and become a several-hundred pound-battering ram flailing in the turbulence—he freed his right knee from the bracing that had held him solidly in the boat. As he reached forward to the grab-loop that would release his neoprene spray skirt and allow the current to tear him free, a sudden stillness in the surrounding water indicated that he and the boat were no longer in the hole; they was drifting downstream at current speed.

Tom reseated his knee, snugged himself back into the bracing, set his paddle, and rolled the boat upright. Even as he shook his head to clear water from his eyes and find his direction to Doug and the safety of the eddy, he was finishing the rolling motion with a powerful stroke forward to give the boat life-saving momentum and speed. Doug's sober comment as they were reunited was that he was very glad not to have seen a friend killed that day.

The two made little of this incident when they rejoined the rest of the group, for it was the exact antithesis of the judgment, skill, and control of our environment that we all sought, Tom and Doug most of all. Luck, not design, had released Tom from that hole just in time, and in our estimation reliance on such luck was the hallmark of the witless thrill-seeker, not the competent outdoor sportsman. We all did make mistakes, of course, as Tom's experience illustrated, and backup systems usually were enough to prevent catastrophe. These included a solid Eskimo roll, equipment that performed flawlessly, and a friend both carrying and skilled with a throw rope.

But such lucky incidents were pushing the odds; they were gifts to be learned from and not willfully repeated. Tom and I privately referred to our "rule of three": If we did not have a solid confidence in doing a move three times in a row, we would not do it at all. We believed a run that left the runner with the thought, "Thank God, I made it! I'll never do that again," was a judgment failure. To my lasting admiration, when we completed our very first run of the Great Falls of the Potomac in 1975, Tom did indeed shoulder his boat, climb up a narrow, blade-shaped center island, and run the route again—twice, for a total of three. I paddled around the pool at the bottom as safety boat, thankful for a cracked seam on my boat.

Nearly a decade after the experience at the Saw Cut on the Aguanus, two laconic entries in Tom's Tsangpo journal summarized days of toil and frustration from opting for a seemingly conservative route:

> *Oct 11 [1998]: ...carry down R. bank but not scouting far enough—realize that bank cliffs out about a mile downstream—1,200-foot climb to get around—camp river R. sandy beach.*
>
> *Oct 12 [1998]: Return to lake dragging boats much of the day—cross to L. bank, hide boats and, carrying 2 days food, climbed around cliffs and camped.*

Most of October 12 was devoted to the backbreaking labor of hauling the hundred-pound boat and gear combinations back upstream. From a position directly beside the train of waves at the bottom of the big rapid, Doug advocated they paddle out across the waves and down to a big eddy by the far left bank. This would avoid not only having to take the difficult trail they had cut around the top of the rapid but also having to traverse the difficult cliffs on the far shore.

Tom and Roger demurred; the maelstrom below, where the main current crashed into cliffs on the left, was too threatening. Without further discussion, Doug acceded to the more conservative estimate and Jamie followed his friend's silent example. We had over the years developed an outlook toward white-water decision-making that we now considered axiomatic, expected of all. If even one person chose to walk around a drop, all others' first responsibility was willingly to assist the bypass, no matter how much extra toil and time it took. We had zero tolerance of peer pressure, even unspoken, for anyone to exceed his comfort zone. The equally important corollary, however, was that the fundamental purpose of our expeditions was to provide opportunities to run white water, and if even one person wanted to run a drop, the others' first responsibility was willingly to assist, particularly with safety. Throw ropes and safety boats were to be put in place; whatever effort and scouting time were required would be provided.

ON THE TSANGPO, THE FOUR PADDLERS WERE LEARNING that this simple principle was still valid, but it applied on a grander scale than at any time in their previous experience. It was imperative that decisions to run be confident and correct; every moment they were on the water they were not far from the lethal edge. Yet decisions not to run could lead to hours and perhaps days of difficult bushwhacking and climbing.

They spent the rest of October 12 returning to their original crossing spot above the rapid and ferrying to the left shore, where they ascended the first cliffs using ropes and pulleys to bring along their gear. There they cached their boats and, carrying bivouac gear and a two-day supply of food, climbed up along a tributary tumbling down from Gyala Pelri and established camp. The evening was dry and wood was plentiful, so Jamie built a larger and more cheerful fire than usual, but they were an exhausted and introspective group that evening.

Doug was impatient with the delay and the overall slow rate of progress. Although he would do everything in his power to avoid pressuring the others to take risks on the water, he knew that success and safety lay in moving lightly and cleanly toward their destination at Rainbow Falls. He was aware that risks also lay in excessive climbing or allowing themselves to become bogged down completely.

Jamie felt keenly the frustration of the wasted time and effort, where Tom and Roger had committed the team to the route down the right without scouting far enough downstream. He admired Doug's calm acceptance of group decisions counter to his own opinion. Ironically, Jamie, the most practiced climber and designer of their climbing systems, had the least desire for a foot expedition. Recorded in his journal were these unvoiced thoughts:

> *And if the hundred foot per mile stretch is impractical, as seems likely, what then? Hike the gorge? Frankly, I'd rather not. I'd rather fly home. But I know I'd lose that vote.*

Roger was the opposite pole. The most conservative on the water, he was also justly confident of the conditioning and stamina of his legs, the one of the four who could most readily hoist his loaded, hundred-pound boat to his shoulder and navigate across the difficult terrain in a single trip. If they had elected to abandon the boats and proceed on foot right from Gyala, he would not have minded.

There was no rancor or discord over these divergent views; usually the four cherished the diversity, and even at the worst moments they bit their tongues and knew that times would soon get better. Tom and I had long felt that the strongest leaders make the best followers. All members of the expedition, paddlers and support, had been selected for their experience and self-confidence: They would speak up when important decisions were being considered and then, as readily, subordinate their own egos—and sometimes fears—to the team decision.

Tom found himself leading, as he wanted, from a middle ground. On the water, he saw numerous instances of brilliant paddling from Doug and Jamie, but he strove to set a more conservative example, avoiding as much risk as possible while the team daily became more accustomed to the river. On shore, he counseled patience with the delays and pacing themselves for a long haul: "Don't force it; we don't have any more energy to expend. We'll find the way."

CHAPTER 6

BACK
IN
TIME

The Gods don't want your litter.

—PEME GOMPA, MONPA HUNTER

HE DAY THAT THE RIVER TEAM, Harry, Doris, and Paulo arrived in Pei and spilled with relief from the vehicles to scout the first rapid, Dave Phillips and I were 35 miles to the north, also exiting our vehicles to examine the first major obstacle on our route to the first resupply point. During my reconnaissance the previous year, the road had wound through cypress forests and bucolic farmsteads along the clear, rushing water of the Rong Chu. Now it ended abruptly in a sheer, 50-foot drop to a streambed choked with talus and tangles of uprooted trees. The floods that still pumped down the Tsangpo had receded on this tributary, but the gashes of landslides, the undercut banks, and the denuded landscape testified to the wanton destruction of August.

Without pause and with barely a glance at the halted trucks or our milling group, a party of a dozen or so colorfully dressed Khampa men and women strode past. They bounded down barely perceptible footholds on the steep, raw-cut bank to the stream, along the boulders, and back up to where the broken road resumed.[1] All carried rice-bag packs and tall bamboo walking staffs. The men wore their long black hair in braids, turned up in a ring around the right ear and finished with a fringe of reddish yarn, and they had long knives with silver sheaths under their belt sashes; a hard stare from one of the men discouraged photography.

Khampas were one thing, but no vehicle had passed this point since August, nor was passage imminent. Roadway workers informed us that this landslide was one of several that had cut the next 11 miles of road. Before the river team even got their boats wet, the support team was already stalled, 18 miles short of the only trail to the rendezvous point.

The drivers from Lhasa were unperturbed. Practiced in conveying tour groups of Westerners around the usual Tibetan destinations, but unused to expeditions and the intensity they require, our crew undoubtedly felt we had traveled far enough to satisfy any adventure traveler. Perhaps we could find a nice monastery to visit or we might rejoin the other party; they had expected all along to sit and drink tea with their friends while the *Ferangis* did whatever Ferangis do.

FORTUNATELY, ANG KAMI SHERPA WAS WITH US. His tall, almost skinny frame, ready humor, and joyful stride under any load or weather belied the fact that this was his 18th major expedition—four of them on Everest. Competent in English, Japanese, and Tibetan, as well as Nepalese and his native dialect, he (and Pemba) had joined us in Kathmandu precisely so we would have present at all times linguists and skilled trekkers who understood and focused on our agenda, and no other. Anticipating challenging times ahead as we depended upon Monpa hunters to reach our destination, I had selected Ang Kami, the older and more experienced of the two, to accompany us.

To Ang Kami, a mere 11-mile gap in the road was but an inconvenience. He and our willing but bewildered guide from the China International Tourism Service (required for all foreign groups) made off smartly on the heels of the Khampas. Soon he returned with porters and ponies (one pony equals two porters per the local pay scale) from a village three miles inside the landslide zone. Cut off from vehicle traffic in both directions, the village's principal industry was now transporting desperate travelers across the barrier, and capitalism was thriving.

We camped in a cow pasture at one end of a short stone bridge connecting us to the village across a small creek. Dave and I joked that perhaps we should sleep that night holding hands, to ensure that neither of us slipped off for unilateral negotiations with the village headman, for here had stood Kinthup's baneful Tongkyuk Dzong.

The following day we followed Kinthup's footsteps down the ravaged valley of the Rong Chu to its confluence with the Po Tsangpo, our route into the heart of the great bend of the Tsangpo. We did so in the bright sun of an October morning, and our pursuers from Tongkyuk were 20 expensive porters porters carrying food and other resupply for the river team. Our route swung uphill, a few hundred feet above the truncated roadbed, and joined a well-trodden, obviously ancient trail contouring the mountainside. Clearly this was the established way before Chinese engineers and their dynamite installed the truck road that so recently had been shrugged off into the streambed. I could imagine Bailey and Morshead approaching around any bend, Morshead sporting six months of beard and in Bailey's words looking "a tramp, and a rather unsuccessful tramp at that." Bailey would be clean shaven, except for a bushy military mustache, but wearing clothes so ragged that when they finally emerged back in India, Morshead would admonish: "We can't travel first class, damn it. Not with you looking the way you do, Bailey."[2]

From the town of Pelung we left the road behind, turning southward on 18 miles of foot trail carved into cliff walls and hillsides. We crossed high above the plunging Po Tsangpo on a cat's cradle of suspension bridges whose ungracious harmonic motion propelled us like a rickety time machine to a land of isolated subsistence villages, feasts of raw takin liver in smoke-blackened caves, and the all-embracing cloud forest. On our first night away from the road, we camped on a white sand beach on the right bank of the Po Tsangpo. A hot spring vented steaming water to form a shallow, hundred-foot lagoon across the red-stained sand, almost boiling hot where it emerged from the bank but icy cold as it merged with the glacial river.

These first three days were rich in scenery and sensation, offering a good trail and an ideal warm-up. I enjoyed introducing my old friend to this area, which I had scouted the previous year, and seeing it freshly through a pair of eyes generally more perceptive than my own. Dave Phillips was not a paddler; our long association was from the military, not white-water sport. This soft-spoken West Virginian had left his home in Gauley Bridge after high school for the broader horizons of the United States Army, and he soon found himself deep in the central highlands of Vietnam, hard by the Laotian border, the senior medic on a Green Beret A Team training Sedang Montagnards. Concluding that the world was a curious place, he spent the next 30 years seeing more of it.

His hair curled slightly by his ears now, the mustache drooped a little beyond the corners of his mouth, and both were pure white against his light-complexioned, sunburned face, but like Bailey he shaved regularly in the field in the military tradition. Behind him lay experience in more than 40 countries, studies at the Army War College, degrees in biology and international relations, and seven published books on Civil War history. And yet, as we panted up a final steep slope from the river and entered the Monpa village of Mendung, overlooking the confluence of the Tsangpo and its tributary Po Tsangpo, he felt as if he had never left his Montagnards.

Fifteen or twenty houses lay scattered along the hillsides, connected by muddy footpaths between low stone walls and rows of banana, peach, and apple trees that delineated roughly plowed fields of corn, onions, cucumber, and vines of scarlet peppers. Passing a cairn of stones and tall prayer flags billowing from 40-foot wooden poles that marked the boundary of the village proper, we made our way directly to the house of Peme Gompa, who had led Tom and me the previous year along Kingdon Ward's route.

Like its neighbors, the house of Peme Gompa stood two stories high, surmounted by a steeply pitched roof of wood shingles to shed the abundant rain. An understory of fieldstone on the uphill side and carved wooden posts downhill supported the main living level above and served as run-in shelter for the family's cattle. The upper floor measured roughly 20-by-20 feet and was sturdily constructed of adze-hewn lumber 3 inches thick, 18 inches wide, and up to 12 feet long. Hinged shutters secured a single unglazed window that let light into each room.

In the large rectangular "great room," where regular family activities took place, a stone-and-clay firebox featured lower holes in which to put firewood and two upper holes on which to set cooking pots. From the open, chimneyless back, smoke rolled upward, filtering through a rack of drying firewood hung from the smoke-blackened ceiling and eventually finding its way out under the eaves of the roof. Furniture was unnecessary. To avoid suffocation by the smoke, all occupants had to sit on the floor or lie down to find enough oxygen to breathe.

The narrow end wall of a small adjacent storage room held a bench upon which sat—on four narrow steps—a brass bell, butter lamps, candles, offering bowls of parched corn, and a set of rectangular, block-printed Tibetan religious mantras. On the wall hung three oversize papier-mâché masks that appeared to represent Deer, Bear, and Something Else, in reddish paint with white teeth and bright contrasting colors. The Monpas brought some peculiar baggage with them when they migrated from eastern Bhutan and the bordering region of Arunachal Pradesh about 200 years before. Above, the space between ceiling and roof served as attics do worldwide: It held several close-woven bamboo baskets of parched corn, a torn basket that might someday be mended, two takin skins on sapling stretchers waiting the next trip to the marketplace at

Pelung, and a large wood-and-hide drum perhaps related to the animal totem masks.

A fat log six feet in length leaned against the elevated entrance deck, cut with steplike notches, which in theory separated the human habitation above from the teeming barnyard below. In practice, this ladder excluded cattle, adult pigs, and most leeches, but it proved no barrier to dogs, cats, the household pet monkey, occasional shoats, and a constant stream of village children.

In his journal Dave Phillips wrote the following on October 8, 1998:

> The people are naturally curious about us and gather in small groups each time we stop to do anything. Like kids everywhere, the little ones are naturally shy. teenagers are openly curious and a bit aggressive with their friendliness. There appears to be no concept of private property and they often pick up and examine anything that raises their curiosity. There is no hint of coveting our materials and I believe they are honest.

Peme Gompa was absent the afternoon when we arrived unannounced, so his eldest son, perhaps age 13, with subtle guidance from his mother proudly made us welcome. The small altar room was graciously provided to Dave and me as a luxurious, private, and smoke-free sleeping area and, more importantly, as a storage area for expedition supplies. Ang Kami Sherpa would bed down on the covered porch, along with our other "staffer."

Lobsang Yunden had appeared as our trucks prepared to leave Lhasa, and he was still with us somewhat against my better judgment. The chief of our guide service explained that Lobsang was not an employee of the company; he needed work, however, and would come along as one of the porters, receiving the negotiated rate when he was needed and otherwise going unpaid. A Tibetan in his mid-20s, about my five-and-a-half-foot height but broader in the shoulders, he spoke what he imagined was English, although it usually required Ang Kami's translation before we understood his meaning. He arrived with only the clothes he wore, a lightweight jacket, a quilted cotton blanket, and a toothbrush, and before we left the last general store behind at Pelung, he begged a salary advance so he could buy green canvas tennis shoes to replace his worn leather street shoes. This all sounded and looked too much like someone's unemployed (and unemployable), citified son-in-law to me, but I really had no grounds to refuse and put up with the situation.

With Ang Kami's guidance we paid off the crowd of porters from Pelung, who then departed back up the trail. Onward progress would now depend on negotiations with our hosts, for throughout Tibet each village does the portering within its own territory, and no union has as firm a hold on the exclusive provision of labor as the village chiefs. Unlike in Nepal where sherpas sign on for the duration of an expedition, here porters carry their loads exactly to the next village, where negotiations begin anew. Bailey and Kingdon Ward both recounted instances of having to change porter teams four or more times in a single day if villages were closely spaced. Here, Mendung and its sister village of Sengchen were the end of the trail, so for the duration of the first resupply to Rainbow Falls, Dave and I would rely solely on the Monpas of Mendung and Sen-

Doug Gordon first paddled with me in 1986 in eastern Mexico. Here, he navigates Tamul Falls, where the Rio Gallinas falls nearly three hundred feet into the Rio Santa Maria, blocking all passage downstream.

DOUG GORDON

JAMIE MCEWAN

ABOVE: After years of anticipation and speculation, the four paddlers finally had hard facts and cold water to test where the road ended at Pei. Slithering like otters down the embankment, they launched onto the Tsangpo.

BELOW: River team leader Tom McEwan and his three companions trained and tested themselves for eight days on the enormous river before deciding to proceed into the heart of the gorge.

JAMIE MCEWAN

The paddlers had to hike forward, sometimes miles, over the gargantuan boulders that comprise the river's shoreline to locate the next safe crossing point before committing themselves to running their boats downstream.

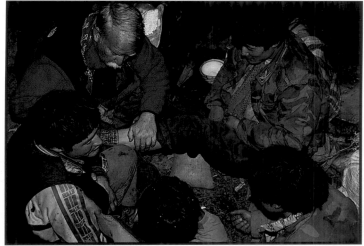

WICKLIFFE W. WALKER

ABOVE: Each day Dave Phillips held sick call, a rapport builder with the Monpas and a practical necessity in seeing that the group stayed healthy and mobile. While checking one patient being treated for a strep infection, Dave found the wound site elaborately traced by the lama with a Sanskrit invocation to Dorje Phagmo, the Diamond Sow.

BELOW: Nourished by monsoon winds sucked up the gorge from the Bay of Bengal, the great old growth cloud forest engulfed the mountain slopes. Pictured across the foreground from left to right are Lobsang Yunden, myself, Roger Zbel, Dave Phillips, and "Village Voice."

JAMIE MCEWAN

ABOVE: Doug Gordon was "first among equals," on this as on previous expeditions frequently leading the way on the water.

RIGHT: Peme Gompa and Tom McEwan used satellite imagery to discuss the route out of the gorge from "Panther Beach." Communication about remote locations was still difficult, but the Monpas found the birds-eye view of the terrain from the satellite more comprehensible than the symbolic representations on topographic maps.

ABOVE: Before leaving the banks of the Tsangpo, Americans, Monpas, and Sherpa gathered for a solemn memorial to our friend, with songs in English and Tibetan, Christian and Buddhist prayer.

BELOW: The panorama beyond the pass above Panther Beach was both awe inspiring and humbling: a sweeping interface of waves of rock and forest, roiling cloud, and glacial ice. Loyal Lobsang Yunden deliberately placed himself immediately in front of myself and Dave Phillips throughout the march, reaching back a remarkably strong supporting arm at every difficult spot.

gchen. If the expedition proceeded farther downstream, Harry and Doris were to leapfrog on down with different villagers, different problems.

At dusk the irrepressible Peme Gompa bounded up the trail from the Po Tsangpo, his face split in a wide grin of surprise and welcome. Any sort of foreign visitor was rare at this edge of the world; it was perhaps unheard-of for someone to repeat a journey like the one Tom and I had made the previous year. Even Kingdon Ward came only once. Peme Gompa quickly shrugged out of the shoulder straps of the woven split-bamboo basket on his back, poured a cup of hot, salty tea from the soot-blackened pot permanently atop the smoldering fireplace, and eagerly asked our plans.

The following morning I entered the quicksand of negotiations with the Monpas, the inscrutable East confronting the unfathomable West with Ang Kami in the middle. Given the difficulty paddlers (and climbers) have in communicating what they do and why, even to family and countrymen ("because it's there"), it is hard to imagine what the Monpas made of us and our enterprise. Theirs was a subsistence society without concepts of disposable income, leisure time, or sport; they seldom bathed, much less thought of getting into a river for pleasure. To the end it remained unclear whether our efforts to explain ourselves, using the overhead satellite photography of the terrain and the picture book Roger had assembled of white-water magazine extracts, had helped or simply deepened the mystery.

Yet in Peme Gompa, the most seasoned hunter and skilled outdoorsman of the group, I did sense a shared joy in the wilderness and the challenge of the unknown, just as I had before with rare individuals in Bhutan and Pakistan. And if he saw in our obsessive quest for rivers some inchoate and difficult pilgrimage, perhaps he understood us better than most of our own countrymen.

Geographic distinctions were mutually unintelligible. Within their own traditional territory, hunters such as Peme Gompa knew every rock and tree, having memorized them under the guidance of their fathers and grandfathers. Beyond, they would admit no knowledge, even if they or other villagers had taken occasional trading (or poaching) trips. Their "cave after three days march below the meadow where the takin gather before migration" meant no more to us than the symbols on our topographic map and GPS coordinates meant to them.

It was not even clear with whom we were bargaining, as the vocal crowd of villagers ebbed and flowed around Peme Gompa's hearth. The village version of a sunshine law was for everyone to crowd into the smoke-filled room. In addition to Peme Gompa, who had led the party the previous year, there was now one very vocal younger man in a rumpled blue suit jacket, his tone assertive and occasionally belligerent. We were still uncertain about his role and status, but we began to hope that "The Village Voice," as he was immediately dubbed by Dave, would not be part of the crew.

Accuracy and veracity were even murkier, because answers seemed a function of at least three sometimes-contradictory variables: what the Monpas thought the interrogator wanted to hear; the respondent's own desires and fears; and occasionally, as in the West, crimes, misdemeanors, or secrets needing concealment. Thus, Harry and Doris had been unable the previous year to proceed downstream beyond the village of Payi, its inhabitants assuring them that the next pass was too deep in snow that first week in November. As they prepared to return along their back trail, a whole family of men, women, and children appeared, having crossed the "snowed-in" pass sockless in their torn canvas Chinese tennis shoes. The good citizens of Payi simply did not want to undertake the journey.

F.M. Bailey recounted an incident at Pemakochung where the residents first told him there was no trail downstream, and then a group of Monpas appeared from that direction. The Monpas agreed to guide Bailey and Morshead to Payi and back to Pemakochung, because that was clearly what Bailey wanted. Two days later the story changed, the Monpas tried to sneak off early in the morning without Bailey and Morshead, and finally they absolutely refused to guide the two Englishmen any farther. Upon finding their own way back to Pemakochung, Bailey learned that their "guides" had robbed the residents there; they had never intended to show the two strangers to their home village or to escort them back to the scene of the crime.

The Monpas believed, of course, that we were infinitely rich and to be charged as much as the market would bear. We believed they were infinitely poor and that probably their only other source of currency that year would be to lead a cow or pig back up the trail to market at the road. Compared with herding cattle across those rickety suspension bridges, accompanying Dave and me to Rainbow Falls should be easy money.

A deal was eventually struck. Peme Gompa assured us that he understood the satellite image, he had been once to Rainbow Falls, and he would guide us there. A total of ten Monpas would accompany us carrying supplies, and they would equip themselves for a 24 day round-trip. Yet even as we shook hands, the very nature of the bargain escaped us all. To Dave, Ang Kami, and me the contract was sealed—unless, of course, events forced us to adapt the plan, in which case we expected the Monpas to be flexible. To our new allies, the contract reflected the circumstances of the moment, and if the relative bargaining positions of the two sides were to change, all bets would be off and negotiations could begin afresh. A curious place indeed.

That evening we sat on the porch of Peme Gompa's house while Dave recorded his thoughts in his journal:

> What a view—sitting near bamboo and banana plants (with a dozen or so cannabis stalks growing between them) and looking out to a pine forest on one ridge with snow-covered peaks in the background. Slopes here begin at 45 degrees and I'm going to lighten my pack.

The sunny day without marching was a rare opportunity to recharge the satellite telephone batteries with our solar panel, and I awaited that evening's scheduled calls with anticipation and frustration. The river team and Harry's support element should be approaching Gyala and the critical decision on how, or if, to proceed. So far I knew only that they were paddling from Pei as planned; I had no details on how it was going.

Absenting myself from that critical test and the decision on proceeding was one of the more difficult leadership choices of the trip. This was the first expedition I had led from shore, rather than from my boat, and every instinct urged me to be there with the river team. Logically, however, I could make no legitimate contribution. In the face of the dangers they would be confronting, only the participants themselves should determine their course, and these were four men in which I had absolute confidence.

If I were there, they might give weight to my opinion, or even to my body language if I stayed silent, while in fact my ten-year absence from paddling made my judgment suspect. Tom, Jamie, Doug, and Roger all had continued growing in the sport, and I had no firsthand knowledge of what they now could or could not handle. In a brief, private conference just before our trucks separated days before, Tom had gently confirmed that my logic, rather than my instinct, was correct: They could handle things at Pei and Gyala. Like it or not, I was now in the role of government and could serve best by defending the shores, delivering the mail, and otherwise staying out of the way.

When Harry's call came as scheduled, precisely at eight that evening, he told me about Jamie's close call and their assumption that the boat was lost forever. This, I knew, did not preclude the other three from continuing on by boat, but it would make that choice more difficult. It also meant that Dave and I would depart in the morning with great uncertainty remaining about the shape of the expedition. As long as the satellite telephones continued working, though, we could accommodate almost any change of plans. If I tipped the scales in favor of doing something in the gorge, even if it were all on foot, that was, unlike the decision on whether or not to boat, a choice I was willing to weigh in on; it was leadership I could and would provide.

Next we ascended one story from the terrace on which Pingso [Mendung] is built to a village called Sengchen on a spur; and then the fun began.

> *We had only one object in coming here—to explore that part of the gorge which had been hidden from us, between the rainbow fall and the Po-Tsangpo confluence, where the river turns back on itself to flow north-westwards round the long jagged spur of Gyala Pelri. Here if anywhere were the 'Falls of the Brahmaputra' which had been a geographical mystery for half a century; and the final solution—falls? or no fails?—was now within our grasp. Our excitement may be imagined; and the fact that the river between the rainbow fall and the confluence dropped 1,851 feet was favorable to the theory of a hundred-foot waterfall somewhere.* [3]

These words were written in 1924 by Capt. Frank Kingdon Ward—the next great Western explorer to enter the gorges after Bailey, a man, in Younghusband's apt phrase, "happy in his vocation and happier still in his choice of the field in which to fulfill it...His object in life is to collect plants...And here in the mountains and the gorges, both in the full flowering season of the year and in the harvest time of seeds, he revels in fulfilling his vocation." [4]—could have come from Dave's journal or my own for October 9, 1998. Like Kingdon Ward's American contemporary Joseph Rock, he was one of the great plant hunters of the early 20th century, commercially sponsored by seed companies to discover new species that could be cultivated in Europe and America. That was but one facet of a remarkable man, however; he was also an explorer, an author, and a World War I veteran who later in life teamed up with the equally legendary Jim (Jungle Jim) Corbett to train

British commandos in jungle survival for operations along the Burma Road during World War II.

By 1924 Kingdon Ward was 38 years old, fluent in Chinese, and a veteran of numerous long expeditions, many of them solo, into the tangle of mountains and rivers where the Eastern Himalaya end and the Yangtze, Salween, Mekong, and Irrawaddy Rivers rise. That year the Earl Cawdor of Scotland joined him for a yearlong collecting trip into the Pemako region, one objective of which was to fill in the blanks on the map left by Bailey and Morshead, including resolving the question of the long-rumored great waterfall on the Tsangpo.

In November 1924 their principal botanical work was done. Plants had been identified and marked when they bloomed in spring and summer, and seeds were collected during return trips in the fall. Starting on Kinthup's and Bailey's routes, with an entourage that included eight female porters and a guru they nicknamed "Walrus," they followed the Tsangpo from Pei to Gyala (Harry and Doris' expedition route); from there, the party went down the right bank past Pemakochung (the river team's expedition route). Near Rainbow Falls, where the river abruptly doubles back to the west around one of Gyala Pelri's great buttresses, they were unable to find a route westward along the right bank, but they did find the route denied to Bailey and Morshead by the deceitful Monpas a decade before.

Crossing overland to the north, they arrived at the village of Payi, 30 river miles downstream from Rainbow Falls, and then began to work their way back up the Tsangpo to fill in the unseen gap (Harry and Doris' reconnaissance route in 1997). At the confluence with the Po Tsangpo, from the village then called Pingso and now Mendung, they took a side excursion farther upstream to glimpse all but about eight miles of the unexplored river (Tom's and my reconnaissance route of 1997).

Kingdon Ward's account from December 12, 1924, continued to reflect perfectly Dave's and my departure from Mendung, including even the weather:

> *The spell of fine weather had come to an end, the sky was overcast, and it was drizzling heavily.*
>
> *Following the hunter's path, we soon entered the forest, at an altitude of about 7,000 feet, and began the steep climb up the ridge. The lower jungle was now left behind, and we entered the temperate rain forest. In the sub-tropical and lower middle rain forest the trees are mixed....*
>
> *This sub-tropical evergreen forest of the lower gorge passes gradually into the deciduous forest of the lower middle temperate belt, which is almost equally varied, but now contains maple, birch, Magnolia, and species of oak. The Rhododendrons met with as we ascend are the 'Arboreum' and the scarlet-flowered 'Irroratum.'*
>
> *Just as some of these trees, particularly the oaks, are beginning to reach gigantic proportions, and to form forests by themselves, we pass at about 8,000 feet into the upper middle rain forest, or temperate rain forest, which is again evergreen. Here the species are few, but they make up in bulk what they lack in variety; for here the very largest trees are found—Rhododendron grande, one of the largest of its kind, and a huge Tsuga, which together make up most of the forest....*

In the upper middle rain forest, the only epiphytes are small Rhododendrons, of which there are at least six species found growing mostly on Tsuga trees, and a white-flowered Coelogyne; one would scarcely expect to find an epiphytic orchid growing here in the snow!

As for this Tsuga, which has the habit of a Lebanon Cedar, it is a giant, probably attaining a height of 200 feet. At intervals along the path we saw shingles and planks, cut by the woodmen and stacked for seasoning; the Tsuga planks measured 15 feet by 8, and were 3 $\frac{1}{2}$ inches thick!

The discovery of this great Tsuga may clear up a certain mystery in Assam, which has long puzzled those connected with the saw-mills in the Sadiya district.

In the year 1900 there was a great flood in the Assam Valley, the origin of which was traced to the Yigrong Lake, by Bailey and Morshead, during their exploration of 1913. During that disastrous affair the swollen Dihang brought down with it besides the bodies of Pobas, logs of Coniferous wood belonging to a species unknown in the Abor Hills. This wood, which is described as strongly scented, soft and light—about 40 lb. to the cubic foot—was sawn up and used in the making of bridges, which twenty-five years later were in an excellent state of preservation; no small triumph in a hot moist climate like that of Assam.

It was not until 1920 that this timber was heard of again. Then, on some of the densely wooded islands of the Brahmaputra, near Sadiya, a number of logs, some of them 12 feet in girth, were discovered half buried by

sand and undergrowth, overgrown with moss, and with-
the heartwood destroyed; but the rest of the wood was
as sound as a bell. These logs also, some of which have
been cut, and others broken off, must have been brought
down by the flood twenty years previously, and stranded
on these low bush-clad islands when the waters
retreated. They were extracted and sawn up, and a vig-
orous search prosecuted for more, and also for the tree
itself, without success. Evidently the tree did not grow
locally, though exploration was carried on for some dis-
tance. There can, I think, be little doubt that the tree
brought down to Assam by the 1900 flood was this Tsuga,
of which I secured some seed.

After ascending the ridge to a height of over 9,000
feet, where the uppermost forest...begins, we started on
a long slanting descent towards the burn, and presently
reached a boulder, beneath which we bivouacked; water
was found some distance down the hillside and brought
up in bamboo tubes. [5]

Kingdon Ward did not remark on one of the most prolific of
all habitats in this wonderland of biodiversity. The steep pas-
tures of mixed grasses and shrub, rising above Sengchen to
meet the forest, seethed with leeches. Whole bushes seemed
to sway in our direction as we passed, dozens of brown and
black pennants waving in our direction like tiny feelers,
attracted perhaps by our heat or smell. Legions of short black
threads hitched their way like inchworms up our walking
poles, thwarted only by chemical warfare when Dave installed
rings soaked with the insecticide nerve agent DEET below the

handles. We donned nylon gaiters provided by a sponsor who doubtless had thought they were to keep our boots from filling with snow, not blood.

Kingdon Ward also did not report how long the walk from Sengchen to the boulder bivouac took himself and Earl Cawdor; presumably the walk was less than the nine hours it took Dave and me. We departed well in advance of the porters that morning, knowing from my experience the previous year that they could catch us at will, tumplines over their foreheads supporting loads of 60 or more pounds in woven bamboo baskets, .22 rifles slung across their chests in case they came across game. To my surprise, first to overtake us was Lobsang, carrying one of the largest rucksacks and still looking as if he had just stepped out of one of Lhasa's seedier night clubs. We were eating a late lunch, perched above the mud on the knobby exposed roots of a gigantic oak tree singled out from its peers by 20 or 30 small prayer flags hung from its lower limbs, various degrees of fading indicating that more than one wayfaring pilgrim hung them there. Lobsang downed his load and politely accepted some trail mix; he sat quietly with us, refusing more food but seemingly concerned to stick with us.

THAT EVENING WE CLUSTERED WITH THE MONPAS around a large, smoldering fire of green rhododendron under the smoke-blackened overhang described by Kingdon Ward, steam rising in equal measure from two teapots balanced on the logs and from the rain-soaked trousers of those nearest the fire. One by one, as hunger overcame cold, men drifted from their places at the fire to rustle around in their packs for dinner. For the Monpas, this was a gray mush produced in their large all-purpose tea bowls by pouring salty tea over tsampa, a ground and roasted barley flour. Sometimes the Monpas mixed the flour with parched corn or enlivened it with small slices of a strong green chili pepper they carried in waterproof wrappings (and proba- bly also used to start campfires in emergencies).

Ang Kami, Lobsang, Dave, and I produced our mush by pouring boiling water, not tea, onto the contents of brightly col- ored foil packets with optimistic names: Chicken Primavera, Hearty Stew with Beef, or Summer Chicken. As we each con- tentedly finished a packet labeled as a meal for two, we care- fully placed the empty packets on the firewood pile to be burned later in the intense hot coals at the center of the fire when every- one went to bed and no longer breathed the smoke. Soon after, we watched in dismay as three Monpas retrieved the packets, examined with animated discussion the bright illustrations of happy campers, mountain climbers, and exotic fruits and veg- etables on the fronts, then sailed them casually over the steep hillside just outside the cave. They disappeared into the heavy underbrush, presumably to last nearly forever in the otherwise decomposing litter of the cloud forest floor.

"Take nothing but photographs. leave nothing but foot- prints" is the mantra of the modern ecotourist and low-impact traveler, and we wholeheartedly agreed with it. Whether in the Canadian wilderness or in other people's backyards, we con- sidered it a matter of principle to leave virtually no sign of our passing. Here, low-impact tourism might offer the inhabitants one of the very few opportunities for economic development that would not destroy their unique culture and magnificent ecosystems. The almost-irresistible pressures of the modern world were already gnawing at the region's frontiers: Lumbering fed Tibet's building industry, and poaching rare wildlife fed the peculiar demands of Asian medicine and superstition.

Ours was a voyage of discovery primarily for ourselves, secondarily for our sport, without pretensions of serving too much of a higher cause; it was neither scientific, economic, nor spiritual. Yet we did hope our efforts would lead to a greater awareness of this magical place and the importance of protecting it, and we sought by example to demonstrate a culturally and ecologically sensitive way to appreciate the place and benefit the economy. Teaching the inhabitants to stop littering their pristine old-growth forest and discouraging them from eating endangered species seemed like a starting place. Tom and I had not been notably successful the previous year with our "green" example, but with Ang Kami's language ability and our better understanding of the culture I hoped for a breakthrough this year.

I tasked Ang Kami with discussing the political incorrectness and economic downside to littering with the three young people who had tossed our food packets over the hillside, and he returned a short time later with a bemused half-smile. It seemed, he reported, that fire was not only a gift of the gods but also a direct gateway to them. Indeed, a common form of Buddhist offering is the burning of tsampa, juniper, or incense. By extension in the Monpa orthodoxy, offerings of burning paint, plastic, and Summer Chicken were frowned upon on "the other side." In fact, the insistence upon burning trash by one of the few previous expeditions passing this way had led to an early snowfall! Later we were to learn that flicking leeches off one's ankles into the fire was particularly egregious, but we never discovered if this stemmed from Buddhism's basic respect for even the least lovable of God's creatures or if it was because the thought of finally arriving to find the Great Beyond also full of leeches was unbearable.

Our actions were worse than those of our climbing predecessors and heroes, who had over years deposited great middens of abandoned oxygen bottles, human waste, and even empty freeze-dried food packets at all the major high camps on the great Snow Goddesses of the Himalaya. We now stood indicted of littering even the Great Beyond. Like missionaries sometimes must, we compromised: We agreed to bury the garbage, and the Monpas promised not to tell the Sierra Club.

CHAPTER 7

DOWNSTREAM

*...ledges from which the gods might quarry
mountains...cliffs where the soaring eagle is
lost to view ere he reaches the summit.* [1]

—MAJOR JOHN WESLEY POWELL

OM, ROGER, JAMIE AND DOUG did not even see their boats on October thirteen. As Harry, Doris and Paulo pulled back 18 miles to the vehicles at Pei to await permission from Tom to drive off for their next task downstream, and Dave and I slogged higher and deeper into the forest 10 miles downstream, the four paddlers set out on foot from their high camp beside the steep side stream on the canyon's left flank. With bivvy gear and two days of food in their rucksacks, a question of tactics, bandied back and forth ever since the long drive across the plateau in the bouncing Land Cruiser, had now been answered in time and sweat: On the Tsangpo they could not simply work their way downstream with their boats, scouting far enough

ahead to ensure escape routes. Too many of those escape routes back upstream would break them. Instead they must scout ahead on foot and, as Tom noted, "never commit the boats until the next way across the river is clear."

Above, wave after wave of ascending vegetation showed the first signs of autumn: Large bushes held masses of yellow berries, and aspenlike trees dropped yellow leaves. Most of the underbrush was still green, but the ferns were brown. Waterfalls poured out of unexpected places high above, then disappeared into foliage again. They found a pothole filled with water beside a stream, tiny dark creatures swimming in its depths.

Ahead and closer to the river, their way lay across barren talus slopes of recent landslides. Choosing his footing as carefully as he could, Jamie nevertheless had a bad moment when a pile of loose rocks, 15 or 20 at once, began to slide beneath his feet. Throwing out his hand to steady himself, he felt the sharp pain of a sprained finger, but he was relieved to feel and hear no further movement above or below.

Beyond the slide zone the wide river flowed swiftly for a half mile, dropped over a low ledge of flat rock, and then banked right into a huge rapid—a series of nearly river-wide white holes proclaiming an obvious carry, even from far upstream. Scrambling over a long jumble of boulders lining the rapid's left bank, the four came to a churning pool where crossing would be possible. They now had a foot route established; they returned upstream to retrieve their boats and work their way back down by paddling where they could and walking where they must.

They had scrambled and climbed that day from 9:00 a.m.

to 6:30 p.m. without stopping. For an hour or longer after supper, Jamie lay awake in his bivvy sack, sharp pain throbbing through a twisted ankle. He had barely noticed it until the agony of his sprained finger and the memory of the rockslide had subsided, and as he silently watched his brother write in his spiral-bound journal by the firelight, he was nagged by doubts about whether he could continue on the injured ankle. A heavy dose of ibuprofen, however, and a silent mantra of "heal, heal, heal" eventually led to a sound sleep and a sore but much better ankle in the morning.

WITH ROPES AND PULLEYS, the paddlers maneuvered their four loaded boats up and around the first set of cliffs, rappelling down after them to river level. After three hard days, they were again beside the large wave train that Doug and Jamie had been eager to cross. Tom and Roger, however, were reluctant to enter it because of turbulence where the river impacted the cliff face. They made camp early and spent the rest of the afternoon stitching torn straps on their packs, a symbolic acknowledgment that backpacking was going to be much more of their future than they had hoped. Jamie, by now the acknowledged team "gear freak," had brought along the needle and waxed thread from a heavy-duty sewing awl, but because he had discarded the handle as too heavy they were forced to take turns awkwardly pushing the needle through the heavy nylon with bare hands and a palm-size rock.

The following day, in Doug's delighted opinion, "had a little of everything." Paddling a short way down the eddy to a point before the next set of cliffs, the four pulled out of the water. Leaving Doug's and Jamie's boats on the shore, they climbed the cliff, hauling Tom's and Roger's loaded boats up with a rope and pulley, lowering them beyond the cliff. Doug and Jamie then climbed back to their boats and prepared to paddle out into the wave train and past the cliff.

Jamie McEwan wrote in his journal on October 15, 1998.

Tom really made me nervous about it, saying how dicey the water was as it came off the cliff.... I felt weak, breathless, clumsy—just the way I do before a race.

Doug went out, first try, looked good. The others were already on the other side, out of sight.

All of a sudden, the radio came alive...in my boat, packed away.... It was Tom telling me not to worry about the rope; they would get it. I wasn't worrying about the rope.

Twice I tried to go out. Violent eddy, plus surf. Twice I tried: the first, swirled around; the second, thought I was on my way, caught a surf on a suddenly breaking wave—and did an inadvertent, sloppy ender. Third try, things opened up, I got to calmer water and sprinted, sprinted, one brace off the reaction wave off the cliff, then into "funny water" where currents met. I was fine there, skirted a hole, made the move.

After the two paddlers rejoined the climbers, Jamie's journal continues:

Then, working our way down the left side. I rarely went first, but did what Doug and Tom did. Roger portaged more often. "King of the Portages," he dubbed himself, and he was good at it—put his boat on his shoulder and carried the whole load off.

ROGER ZBEL WAS AN UNLIKELY CONSERVATIVE. He had grown up in the Washington, D.C., area but had no early exposure to the burgeoning white-water community there. The summer after he graduated from high school, he was working construction and not thinking much about the future. Then, he and a high school friend were invited to try white-water canoeing. Two "experienced" friends led them and a borrowed 17-foot aluminum canoe to Smoke Hole Canyon in West Virginia, one of the headwaters of the Potomac.

Even at summer's low water levels, this intermediate run would hardly be considered the place to initiate two beginners, but low water was not what they found at the put-in point. Overnight thunderstorms had pumped the river up, its speed evident from the passing logs and deadfall picked up from its banks. After a leisurely truck-stop breakfast while waiting vainly for the flow to become less daunting, Roger and his friend accepted the assurances of their veteran guides: "Just follow us; you'll be all right."

They were not all right. The aluminum canoe soon crunched sideways into a rock, tipped upstream, and filled with water, spilling its occupants into the brown flood. The force of the current quickly flattened the boat and wrapped it securely around the immovable rock, where it would remain, resisting all efforts to extricate it with ropes and pulleys even after the water level dropped. Both swimmers eventually clawed their way to the bank, far downstream. His friend never again set foot in a canoe, even on flat water. Roger, however, had found his life's work.

THE 1970S AND EARLY 1980S WERE YEARS OF TRANSITION, a coming of age, for white-water sport. The small, exclusively European racing aspect of the sport of the 1950s had been embraced in the 1960s by American paddlers, who were initially drawn to running rivers as an outgrowth of camping, fishing, and wilderness appreciation. Few trained daily or year-round. They met and camped beside white-water rivers on weekends, teaming up to hang slalom gates on Friday afternoon or Saturday morning before racing in boats that most of them had built in their garages.

Beginning in 1961, the United States sent a small team to Europe every other year for the biannual World Championships, and slowly we brought back more sophisticated training methods and boat designs. Through the 1960s, however, the sport remained small, clubby, and more hobby than discipline on both sides of the Atlantic. When the dominant Europeans, lead by the West Germans, nominated white-water slalom to be included for the first time at the Munich Olympics in 1972, that world was transformed.

Competition for the slots to compete in the Olympics and World Championships rapidly became intense. For the first time, contenders left schools and jobs to train exclusively, and when Jamie McEwan brought one of the precious Olympic medals back to America the direction for the next generation of competitors was set. No less than in other mainstream sports, competition at elite levels became a full-time occupation, with coaching staff, multiple workouts daily, summers on the World Cup circuit in Europe, and winter training in southern California or Costa Rica. By maintaining a regular career, Doug Gordon was an exception. But for "the quest," he, too, postponed pursuing a doctorate and sacrificed professional opportunities for more than a decade.

Another full-time white-water occupation was emerging at the same time, far from the world of elite racing. Rafting had for decades been limited almost exclusively to floating tourists down the Grand Canyon of the Colorado, the Snake, and a few other big western rivers in large, guide-rowed rafts. In the 1970s, up and down the Appalachians a different type of rafting gradually emerged, with smaller rafts better adapted to the smaller, steeper rivers, paddled by the customers themselves with a guide's assistance. As the popularity of outdoor sports burgeoned, rafting companies and kayaking schools were founded within reach of large cities, providing raft guides and instructors with the first widespread opportunities to make a living from the sport.

Roger was a link between the phenomena of racing and rafting, and yet he remained apart from both of them. By the spring of 1981, he was living outside Albright, West Virginia, in a former one-room schoolhouse named "Moon Base Alpha" because it sat at the center of a vast strip mine with denuded hills like moonscapes in every direction. Roger's construction employment was now reduced to two or three months a year, just enough to supplement a raft guide's income so he could boat the rest of the year. Late that summer, he and partner Phil Coleman founded Precision Rafting Expeditions in nearby Friendsville, Maryland, on the Youghiogheny River.

IN THE 1970s AND EARLY 1980s. Albright and Friendsville became the twin foci of an emerging group of white-water iconoclasts: rafting guides and boat builders who lived, worked, and played on the white-water rivers of West Virginia and Maryland, who knew their home rivers as intimately as the racers knew their training courses. Flaunting a hard-paddling, hard-living image, they challenged the conventional dicta of the paddling establishments, both East Coast and West, and literally added a new dimension to white-water sport.

Conventional paddlers, myself very much included, then viewed rapids from the more-or-less horizontal surface plane, and we saw and used currents of differing speeds to propel us on our chosen routes. The vertical flows we regarded primarily as obstacles to downstream travel—waves that slow our progress as moguls slow a downhill skier, recirculating holes that could slow or stop or pitch a boat end-over-end, downward flows that could plunge a swimmer into a dark, airless, and hostile regions.

Capitalizing on radical new boat designs, techniques, and thinking introduced by World Champion slalom canoeists Jon Ludbil and Dave Hearn in nearby Washington, D.C., the Albright counterculture embraced that vertical dimension. With specially designed kayaks, they taught themselves to paddle on the upward- and downward-flowing currents, deliberately plunging the ends and sometimes their entire boats deep underwater, for the first time paddling the whole river rather than the surface plane. They called this new freestyle discipline "squirt boating": When placed perfectly between two powerful currents, a boat could be shot upward like a watermelon seed pinched between forefinger and thumb. A decade later this was to be one of the foundations of the popular new competition of white-water rodeo.

Despite his instinctive and highly trained "feel" for moving water and the enormous self-discipline to train to national team levels on his own, Roger's brief flirtation with the world of sanctioned, organized white-water racing did not come to much. At the selection trials for the U. S. Wildwater Team in 1988, much of the established downriver racing world regarded the blond-bearded interloper with suspicion. The evening before the final selection trials, the national team coach singled him out in a competitors' meeting, declaring that Roger had the worst style he had ever seen. Such a frosty reception was not extended by everyone, however. A friendly camaraderie was offered by two veteran slalom competitors who—for a change of pace—were racing wildwater that year in a two-man canoe: Lecky Haller and his partner, Jamie McEwan.

From sheer cussedness Roger nailed down the final slot on that year's U. S. Team and prepared for his first and last big international race. The following year the World Whitewater Championships were to be held on the Savage River in upper Maryland, not far from Friendsville, so in 1988 all the world's best came to race and rehearse on the slalom and wildwater courses. Wildwater racing since its inception has been dominated by European specialists, and the men's kayak race is by far the most competitive class in the competitions. Roger was under no illusions that he would be able to place highly without years of training and experience devoted to this one discipline. His personal, unannounced goal, he will now admit with a shy smile, was to beat all the European women (he did by an uncomfortably small half-second margin) and go back to the Appalachian rivers he loved.

While Tom, Jamie, and I were seeking out a wide variety of rivers in North America, Europe and Asia, Roger and the rest of the small group of radicals were back in the hills of

Appalachia. Beholden to no one, they were largely unknown to the rest of the white-water community and finding ever more difficult challenges on their home rivers. They began a series of small, invitational, unsanctioned races down rivers considered too difficult for conventional wildwater racing, or even for World Championships. From a ragged beginning in 1981, with a dozen paddlers racing down the upper Youghiogheny River near Friendsville for T-shirt prizes, these races slowly expanded to West Virginia's Gauley River, Kentucky's Russell Fork, the Great Falls of the Potomac, and the Gore Canyon of the Colorado. And for a decade and a half, the most successful competitor in any class was Roger Zbel in the men's kayak.

Instigated by Roger's business partner, Phil Coleman, an even smaller group was also testing the limits of running rivers in flood. Slowly building their confidence on successively higher water levels, they eventually were running rivers when flows were three, four, and five times the level at which commercial rafting was cut off as too dangerous. On cold, rainy days in early spring, when tourists stayed home and even serious white-water paddlers bypassed the flooded standard runs to seek out smaller creeks and easier rapids, Roger, Phil, the Snyder brothers, and the rest of their tiny fraternity were making runs unmatched to this day, completely unnoticed by the paddling magazines or the wider boating world. To those of us who knew what Roger was doing, he was anything but "King of the Portages."

By 1998, though, like the rest of us Roger had a family. Just before departing for the airport, Roger had squatted, looked four-year-old Cari eye to eye, and promised her and her mother,

Nancy, that he would come home all right. That was not a promise he would risk breaking, not for any price.

LATE IN THE DAY the tired paddlers came to a final, long carry. Hauling their heavily laden boats over a shoreline strewn with boulders 20 and more feet in height, like Arctic explorers hauling hundred-pound sledges through fields of upthrust ice, they painstakingly made their way for several hundred yards around an unrunnable drop. Just beyond, as if a reward for their efforts, an idyllic campsite overlooked the sweeping river from a flat grassy shelf 200 feet above. The site was a benevolent refuge from the vicious, unstable rockslides, the casually indifferent power of the river, the inhuman scale of the mountain slopes. They found no sign of man—no fire-blackened ring of stones, no spike of bamboo lopped off by a passing machete.

Jamie rigged a pulley from a tree to haul up the laden boats, showing off a bit by configuring carabiners and rope into a ratchet-like system that allowed the heavy loads to be raised without slipping back between pulls. The four swiftly selected sites around the grassy ledge for their bivvy sacks and for the fire, then turned to collecting firewood and stringing a rescue rope between scattered pine trees as a drying line for wet clothing and gear.

All were tired but elated by the day's downstream progress, and none was more so than Tom. He felt that a weight had been lifted from his shoulders after they had worked out the way to move forward—"the system." In hindsight, perhaps it should have been obvious, but in fact the four experienced expedition paddlers had taken all these days to reach consensus. They would take no further shortcuts. Every foot of their route would

begin with a "global scout:" From each crossing spot, they would
hike forward on foot all the way to the next spot, down both
banks if necessary. Only then would they perform the "local
scout" to work out an exact route with boats, identifying which
sections could be paddled, which ones carried or rock-climbed.
Finally they would bring along the boats, then repeat the process
to the next crossing spot.

With this breakthrough, Tom could feel much of the tension and frustration in their group psyche melt away, and for
him personally much of the leadership burden lightened. He
resolved in the morning to step back and enjoy his surroundings. He would also resume shooting video, which he had neg-
lected for the past three days while urgently getting the team
back on track. In a quiet aside with Doug, the two discussed
the four days of frustration followed by this day of encouragement. "If we don't force it," Tom allowed, "we'll start to see
steady progress now that we've found 'the system.' "

As EVENING'S LONG SHADOWS CHILLED THE RIVER BOTTOM even while
bright sun reflected off the heights above, Tom opened the
antenna lid from the Inmarsat to a 45-degree angle, aligned it
with his compass to point toward the satellite that hovers over
the Indian subcontinent, and cut their ties to Harry. The support team, which had remained between Gyala and Pei just in
case the group on the river needed further assistance, would
now embark on their next phase, following Dave's and my
route by vehicle and foot to the Po Tsangpo-Tsangpo confluence to assist from below. Tom, Roger, Jamie, and Doug were
on their own, committed to meeting Dave and me at the next
resupply point downstream, near Rainbow Falls. The next day,

they calculated, they would cross the symbolic line directly between the peaks of Namcha Barwa and Gyala Pelri, more than 16,000 feet down in Earth's greatest canyon.

CHAPTER 8

NEVERLAND

Wendy: *"But where do you live mostly now?"*
Peter Pan: *"With the lost boys."*

That, Peter had told Wendy, was the way to the
Neverland; but even birds. carrying maps
and consulting them at windy corners, could not
have sighted it with these instructions.[1]

—J.M. BARRIE, *PETER PAN*

CTOBER 10. when the paddlers did their last rehearsal and performed for Paolo's camera at the "Video Rapid," was also a light day for Dave and me 4,000 feet above the river on our trek toward Rainbow Falls with the river team's resupply. The tentless Monpas were limited to traveling from one protective overhang to another in their traditional hunting patterns; they informed Ang Kami that the next shelter was no more than a half day away, but the following day would be long and hard indeed. Under gloomy overcast skies, we cut downhill on a slippery trail through heavy rhododendron and forest that "can only be described as '*enchanted,*' " as Dave wrote in his journal.

While the floor is sloped, filled with leaf litter and boulders, the enormous trees—three and four feet in diameter and one hundred feet tall—have a beauty that is enhanced by thick coatings of moss, epiphytes (probably orchids and bromeliads). Many of the moss clusters have become so thick that layers have decomposed to form soil, and ferns are growing in it—high above the forest floor where they normally grow. Fallen trees lean against the living and their moss-covered skeletons add to the artist's scene surrounding all of us.

The rain-slicked trail showed evidence of hunters' use, and two exceptionally steep pitches were made navigable by stairlike notches hacked into great, nearly vertical logs. While the Monpas with their cumbersome baskets and ragged tennis shoes proceeded easily, Dave and I slipped and fell with regularity on the wet moss underfoot, despite carbide-tipped fiberglass walking sticks and lightweight backpacks engineered to balance their wearers. Having exhausted my vanity here the previous year, I asked Ang Kami to carry the indispensable satellite telephone, which he cheerfully added to his 80-pound pack and safeguarded throughout the trip.

Behind me I heard a sound like that of a line drive heading for the bleachers, and I turned to find Dave already kneeling over a semiconscious Lobsang. A ragged scalp of moss, peeled off a tree trunk lying across the trail, indicated the impact point of Lobsang's head, and Dave told me with concern that Lobsang had been completely out when he had reached him. Within minutes the embarrassed Lobsang was insisting he was fine, shrugging into his pack straps and resuming his place

walking between Dave and me, while Dave and I soberly contemplated the implications of having to carry someone with
even a minor injury out of this terrain.

Our way led down to a glacial torrent, born of the vast
snowfields of Gyala Pelri high above our right shoulders and
dropping at a frightening angle into the Tsangpo thousands of
feet below our left feet. These words from Kingdon Ward's
journal could have been our own:

> *Descending steeply to the burn, which flowed from one*
> *of Gyala Pelri's blunt-nosed glaciers, we crossed by a*
> *fallen tree, and turned up a rocky glen on the other side.*
> *At an immense block of stone so perched on the slope as*
> *to afford shelter to a platoon, a halt was called...* [2]

Where Kingdon Ward had reported a fallen tree, we found three
parallel tree trunks, laced together by strands of split bamboo
so they would not roll, spanning the channel between rock
ledges. Otherwise the scene was unchanged from 1924. We
crossed, placing our feet carefully, tap-tapping with our walking sticks for balance, and concentrating on how good this would
look in photos to avoid thinking about the results of a slip.

Under the "immense block of stone" Dave and I immediately changed into dry fleece from waterproof sacks inside our
packs, made coffee, and began to rest our legs for the next day,
but for the Monpas the early afternoon camp was a chance to
catch up with routine chores of the hunt. Several of the younger
ones quickly shed their packs, loaded .22 rifles, and disappeared
up the trail. One man spent hours hewing a wooden trough to
catch water dripping from the roof of the rock shelter and elim-
inate the need to carry water from a distant spring. Peme Gompa

produced an ax head from his pack and spent the afternoon
fashioning a hardwood handle, presumably from a tree best
found at this locale. On the trail and in the caves, day by day
the personalities of the Monpas emerged. Peme Gompa at 44
was the eldest, the most experienced hunter, and the leader in
all route finding. With the exception of The Village Voice in his
mid-30s, the others were relative youngsters, from perhaps 30
down to 12. Dave dubbed them the "Lost Boys" and assigned
nicknames to fix them in our minds: In his journal he wrote
the following:

> *"The Village Voice"...the lead negotiator when talks
> were held over daily rates of pay, a long session that left
> us in doubt about both his sincerity and general relia-
> bility.... We were not pleased to have him along....*
>
> *"Squad Leader"...When he was on the same planet
> as the remainder of the party, he was an effective leader
> of the small group of the youngest of the porters. When-
> ever he became angry—and he was often angry—his
> ability to hold saliva in his mouth was significantly
> reduced.*
>
> *"Pointman"...always the first to catch up and pass
> us whenever we tried to get an early start...
> one of the youngest of the porters, carried a .22 rifle—
> along with his basket and tumpline.... His olive drab
> Chinese army raincoat gave him a distinctly military
> look reminiscent of Montagnard tribesmen on patrols
> along Viet Nam's border with Laos.*
>
> *"Hummer"...a slender fellow having darker,
> non-Monpa features said to be associated with the Lopa
> tribe...generally, and occasionally irritatingly, hummed*

*a constant low religious mantra, and in the silence
around the fire we could hear him very plainly.*

*"Baby-san"...the youngest, at about twelve or thir-
teen and on his initial trip into the deep forest...liable, but
cannot resist pilfering "Think Bars" from our supplies.*

*"Chaplain"...probably older than his smooth,
round face implies...performs religious rites for
the group, armed with a small brass bell and a set of
block-printed texts, dressed in a well-worn Chicago
Bulls sweatsuit.*

*"Redford"...indeterminate age between twenty-two
and thirty-two...close to Peme Gompa...a handsome
fellow with features that made him resemble an Asian
Robert Redford.*

EACH DAY DAVE HELD SICK CALL. a rapport builder with the
Monpas and a practical necessity in seeing that the group
stayed healthy and mobile. With Ang Kami's soft-voiced
interpretation, he listened to any new health complaints, followed up on those he was already treating, and passed out
single doses of medication as required. All suffered secondary infections in leech bites around their ankles, and antibiotic ointment was in high demand.

Redford had developed a severe limp during the afternoon's
march, so Dave summoned a conference with him, Peme
Gompa, and Ang Kami. He discovered that what had started as
the ubiquitous infected leech bite on Redford's left ankle had
become, in the constant damp and unsanitary conditions, an
unusually shaped, whorled, and pus-filled ulcer, probably a
strep infection. There was associated swelling and tenderness

in the lymph nodes of his left groin. Left untreated, this was likely to get rapidly worse, might compromise further progress if Redford had to be carried out, and might even compromise the young man's leg.

After cleaning the infected ankle carefully, Dave spread a strong antibiotic ointment over the infection site and an antiseptic solution on the surrounding area. A systemic antibiotic like oral penicillin was also required to curb the spread of the infection into the soft tissues, though, and he discovered that Redford had never swallowed a tablet of any kind. With some coaching from Ang Kami, and a shot of salty Tibetan tea that would have made Dave or me gag, Redford got down the first 500-mg tablet.

It was important that Redford take the full course to completely clear up this strep, and long experience as a field medic had taught Dave that simply issuing him 28 tablets would be fruitless. He had many times seen patients abandon their medicine when no result was visible after the first pill; if a tablet's magic didn't work, they thought the medicine was worthless. Dave had seen bottles of pills immediately handed out, one to everyone in a village, so all could share the magic. He had even seen pills strung onto amulets for longer-lasting curative powers. He resolved to keep an eye on Redford and personally administer each tablet, four per day for a week.

DURING OUR EVENING TELEPHONE CHECK with Harry's base camp, Tom reported the recovery of Jamie's boat and their planned departure the following day, bound for Rainbow Falls with 15 days of food. Although our destination was now clear, major questions remained about both the river and the land routes.

Where Kingdon Ward in 1924, and Tom and I in 1997, had descended to river level, our path the following morning diverged, leading upward and farther upstream. As we traversed one section of trail across a steep rock-and-grass slope, a rent in the bank of clouds on our left briefly revealed the Tsangpo more than 2,000 feet below, the rumble of one big rapid distinctly audible. Down there Kingdon Ward had determined his position, eight miles downstream from Rainbow Falls and four miles upstream from the confluence at Gompo Ne, and measured the elevation of the river. Unable to proceed far upstream or down, he retraced his steps leaving those eight- and four-mile gaps still blank on the map. He concluded, however, that he had enough data to answer his own question— "falls? or no falls?"—with at least an educated guess:

> ...there is a legend current amongst the Tibetans, and said to be recorded in certain sacred books kept in the monastery at Pemakochung, that between the rainbow fall and the confluence there are no less than seventy five of these falls, each presided over by a spirit—whether benevolent or malicious is not stated. Supposing that to be more or less true, and supposing each fall or rapid to be only 20 feet high, the difference of height is easily accounted for. [3]

The great explorer's negative estimate put to rest speculation over the "Falls of the Brahmaputra" for 80 years, until two different speculations in the 1980s drew us and others to resume the quest. If the text at Pemakochung and Kingdon Ward's analysis were correct, then a series of 75 rapids and falls of 20 feet each would indeed be an earthly paradise for white-water sportsmen (except in high water, of course). But in Kathmandu, Buddhist scholar and Tibetan linguist Ian Baker was on the trail of contradictory sacred texts, which did hint at a high waterfall of great symbolic and religious import, and this trail led him, Hamid Sardar of Harvard, and a few other companions on repeated exploratory treks into the gorges starting in 1993. Kingdon Ward's blanks on the map still remained unexplored in 1998, though, and Ian, Hamid, and Ken Storm of Minneapolis were to commence their latest effort in just two weeks, also sponsored by the National Geographic Society. The two expeditions could conceivably overlap near Rainbow Falls, although we would be approaching from opposite directions, physically and philosophically.

OVER THE NEXT TWO DAYS OF STEADY ASCENT through a cold and continuous rain, the forest became coniferous, then gradually thinned to isolated groves interspersed with thick tangles of low alpine bushes and grasses. The nearly constant rains and summer's snowmelt saturated a thin layer of peaty black soil on the solid bedrock, producing muskeg bogs on every level bench. We were now in the prime territory of the takin, a wild, blue-eyed bovine somewhat resembling a musk ox. The hunters perked up and began eyeing the high meadows whenever gaps in the low-hanging clouds allowed, for this creature was their favorite prey.

Evening's camp under the next rock ledge played out the now familiar but still surreal scene, illuminated by ropy branches of rhododendron coaxed to smoky flames with a bellows made from a short length of pipe and the remains of a Peoples Liberation Army raincoat. A constantly shifting population formed two rows around the fire, those in front sitting as long as they could tolerate the intense heat and smoke, those behind standing as long as they could tolerate the cold at their backs and seeping water dripping off the roof onto their heads. Dave nodded half awake, listening to Hammer's droning mantra echoed by the rain drumming on a nylon tarp rigged to extend the shelter's overhang. One of the young men, face shadowed near the back, began a folk song, unintelligible but attractive. As the clear, high tenor faded after the third verse, Pointman joined in pure, unaccented idiom: "Baaaaad to the bone!"

After enjoying Dave's initial shock, I explained that Pointman had also been with us the previous year, and Tom had spent the evenings sharing songs, American and Monpa, with the delighted boys. Dave gleefully began teaching them how to perform high fives with which to greet the paddlers when we rendezvoused at Rainbow Falls. "Take nothing but pictures, leave nothing but footprints" indeed. He wished the next passing anthropologist luck in sorting that out.

STILL IN A STEADY, COLD RAINFALL, OUR WAY WOUND UP over another small pass and down into a large bowl, which gathered dozens of steep streams of water from almost a 270-degree arc of surrounding rocky ridges 3,000 and more feet above our heads. Due north and below eye level lay clouds, concealing a precipitous plunge of rock and water to the Tsangpo far below. If frozen, geomorphologists would have called this bowl a hanging glacier; instead it was a hanging bog, the nearly flat floor knee-deep in water, punctuated by hummocks and islands of tallgrasses and bushes resembling alder. When clouds concealed the heights above and the depths below, we could as well have been in the wilderness of Quebec, except for the lack of beaver.

Here lay Nadang, which like most of Pemako can be vastly different things to different beholders. The Monpas described it as a "summer village," but we saw no evidence of huts or the stone walls that Tibetan herders use with tent roofs for summer-pasture camps. Nadang also was reportedly remarkable for a number of sacred shrines, hidden from all but the particularly enlightened pilgrim. Soaked to the waist, we were grateful simply to shelter for the night at the small but dry overhanging ledge.

With a couple hours of daylight left, the Monpas departed for takin hunting and other missions. Ang Kami, Lobsang, Dave, and I resorted all the supplies, lightening the onward loads by caching food supplies deep in the back of the cave, covered by a tarp, for the return journey with the paddlers.

We were not vouchsafed a view of the hidden temples; indeed, whole cathedrals could have been concealed within the persistent clouds hanging low in the Nadang bowl, but magic was all around us, nevertheless, when we resumed our upward trek the following morning. Coming to one of the numerous small, gravel-choked streams rushing down the valley from a glacier dimly visible through the fog, Squad Leader encouraged us to wash our faces, sip some water, and then cross. On the far side, we performed a full face wash and hair rinse before continuing. Squad Leader's eager smiling pantomime did not make clear how this stream differed from those we had been unhappily soaking in for the previous three days, but the whole ritual seemed to be concerned with invoking good weather, perhaps by demonstrating that we were now wet from head to foot.

By evening's firelight, Dave checked Redford's infected ankle and found remarkable improvement: There was no remaining inguinal node involvement, and the skin was now 90 percent intact where pus-filled whorls had been before. Even more remarkable, the entire wound site and surrounding area were now elaborately traced with Sanskrit, an invocation to Dorje Phagmo scribed by Chaplain with a black, felt-tipped pen. Perhaps it is no coincidence they are called Magic Markers. Combining modern medicine with traditional healing practices is now trendy, and Dave began to fantasize about a submission to the Journal of the American Medical Association.

WITH THE WEATHER IMPROVING AND EVERYONE HEALTHY, the next morning was the time for acquiring a takin for the larder. Chaplain placed freshly picked, fragrant green herbs, handfuls of tsampa flour, and rancid butter on the fire. He then rang a small brass bell and chanted mantras as Squad Leader tossed cups of tea to the four corners of the camp and Pointman and Baby-san carried pans of hot coals and smoking tsampa 30 yards down the trail in each direction. The younger men took off an hour in advance of our main body to cut trail for us, but their primary purpose was to hunt before the game was alerted.

We never got a clear explanation of the dispensation that allowed these Buddhists to gleefully hunt and kill the takin. Sometimes it seemed that the takin was a special animal, specifically created for the table, so that killing it was not the same as the proscribed killing of other creatures. Other times it seemed that because any creature, man or beast, that died in the sacred land of Pemako was instantly freed from the wheel of life and achieved nirvana, killing anything was in fact doing it a favor. (That they shot goral, pheasant, and other game with equal alacrity argued toward the latter theory.) Dave and I concluded that probably the Monpas themselves were unclear about this theological nuance; that this was likely an uneasy accommodation of customs and economics that long predated Buddhism or even Bon.

We were now well above the boggy floor of the bowl, where the sides began to steepen; nearly vertical, bare rock faces ringed us thousands of feet above. Like a Chinese landscape painting, the heavy rain clouds had dissipated to narrow lenses drifting within the bowl, revealing dozens of rivulets coursing down the steep sides in countless waterfalls. Each narrow streambed doubled as a rocky avalanche chute, with alternately polished bedrock and unstable piles of broken rubble, separated by V-shaped wedges of thin soil supporting alpine grasses and brush, thickets of dwarf rhododendron, and isolated groves of stunted coniferous trees.

The previous day we had heard a substantial avalanche ahead, and in one gully we now crossed its aftermath, the loose rocks covered with a fine-powder residue like a quarry face after blasting. Lobsang began positioning himself just in front of Dave and me in crossing each steep chute, feeling his way across and reaching back a surprisingly strong hand at each tricky spot. At one steep, slippery traverse we placed a fixed rope for the first time on the trip.

In the early afternoon we halted at the junction of two gullies, where two gargantuan boulders perched 20 feet high, their generously overhanging sides providing relatively luxurious accommodations. On their flat tops, a verdant cap of grass and low bushes hanging like bangs down their sides indicated that years, perhaps generations, had passed since their spectacular roll down to this location. The Monpas downed loads in the larger cave, while Ang Kami, Lobsang, Dave, and I moved into the smaller one for a rare bit of relative privacy.

The Monpas eagerly scanned the hillsides above, soon spotting several takins, which minutes later with careful coaching we could also see. Groups of three and four brownish animals grazed 500 to 1,000 feet above our heads. When alarmed, they bounded down the gullies and draws we had hesitated to walk across. Now for the first time, instead of sending out the boys on their own, Peme Gompa led one hunt, Village Voice another, leaving behind only Chaplain to tend the fire.

A loud hail from the trail two hours later heralded the arrival of Pointman and Squad Leader, wide grins on blood-streaked faces, each with a skinned haunch wrapped in a rubberized raincoat and slung across his back with rope shoulder straps. The rest of the elated crew filtered in over the next hour, bearing the various parts of what had probably been a 200- or 300-pound takin. Peme Gompa bounded in last, the black takin's head staring resignedly out of his pack basket, blue eyes set between short curled horns like those of a small water buffalo.

Chaplain and Baby-san quickly stoked up the fire, and the evening evolved into a repast seemingly out of the Stone Age. Instigated by Squad Leader, the youngsters passed the raw liver around hand to bloody hand, seizing chunks in their teeth and cutting them off with their short belt knives. Peme Gompa roasted the heart and testicles and offered us portions as special delicacies. Finally everyone settled down to gorging on barely roasted rib and back meat, tossing strips directly onto the coals and branches in the fire, then contesting who could pull them out again with bare fingers and without complaint.

Dave and I whittled wimpy barbecuing sticks and roasted thin strips of the surprisingly tender, flavorful tenderloin, and near the back of the crowd Lobsang enjoyed a share of ribs. Ang Kami politely accepted a few tastes, then silently watched with his frequent, bemused half-smile. When we four retired to our separate cave about nine that night, the feasting and boisterous talk seemed just begun.

Somehow the next day became, without discussion, a rest day. The Monpas were less than eager to climb all day gorged on fresh meat, but serious work also needed to be done to preserve the portions of the takin not consumed. A ten-foot center pole, surmounted by the drying skin scraped clean of fat and flesh and stretched on a frame of saplings, leaned above the smoky fire and supported an elaborate lattice of saplings and thinly sliced smoking meat. Directly over the fire from a string hung the gallbladder, evidently of great medicinal value.

On a log with one side flattened to make a cutting board, one young man chopped meat finely with his machete. Another, with both hands nearly to the elbow in a pot of mixed blood and water, kneaded in the chopped meat, tsampa, and chilies. A third stuffed the washed intestines with the concoction, knotted them neatly into two-foot link sausages, and dropped them into a pot of boiling water. Peme Gompa mixed tsampa into a dough, which he molded over small meatballs to form *momo*, a Tibetan dumpling, and boiled in yet another pot. A portion of this bounty was packed for the onward journey, while the remainder, including the skin, was cached in the back of the cave for our return. It was a long walk back, and little but the skin would remain uneaten by the time they got back to Mendung; it was easy to see why this was about the practical limit of their hunting area.

SOMEWHAT TO MY SURPRISE, CN THE MORNING OF OCTOBER 16 Peme Gompa led the way directly upward from our bivouac, plainly heading south rather than continuing to contour around to the east in the direction of Rainbow Falls. From this height we could see a rocky saddle about 2,000 feet above, at between 12,000 and 13,000 feet elevation the lowest point of the surrounding rim, and evidently this was his chosen route to exit the bowl we were in. It would place us on the southern flank of the great buttress of Gyala Pelri that forced the Tsangpo's dramatic switchback at Rainbow Falls.

While trivial by the standards of Himalayan mountaineers, including Ang Kami, the altitude was now enough to slow Dave and me to a trudge, while the Monpas took regular cigarette breaks to avoid getting too far ahead. Bare rock became more frequent and even steeper, and twice Peme Gompa and Ang Kami fixed ropes for the security of the rest of us. Five hours of this slow upward progress brought us finally to the narrow saddle, and in a chill wind we gazed around in wonder.

Behind us to the north, the waterfall-etched bowl dropped away to the cloud-choked valley of the Tsangpo at the lower end of the inner gorge. Beneath our feet to the south forested mountainside dropped precipitously 3,500 feet, also to the Tsangpo but 19 river miles upstream. Across the river we could see the rounded terrace about 1,000 feet above the river where the abandoned monastery of Pemakochung had formerly been located. Beyond, invisible in heavy cloud, Namcha Barwa was nevertheless a looming presence.

The Monpas were rested and ready to drop down out of the wind when Dave and I crested the pass. Before they could shoulder their loads and move on, however, I insisted to Ang Kami that we must have a short conference with Peme Gompa to assuage my vague concern about the direction of the onward route. Village Voice and Squad Leader came over as well, and it was quickly evident that the atmosphere was different, the easy camaraderie of the takin feast and folk songs replaced by a sullen unease. Village Voice did most of the talking; Peme Gompa remaining largely silent as if he had not the right to speak for the group. This was as far as they had ever traveled, they now told Ang Kami; the only trail beyond led upstream to Gyala and Pe, 20 days over dangerous high routes. They could probably find a way directly down to the river, but proceeding farther downstream was impossible.

The implications of our crew's Jekyll and Hyde transformation were unpleasant, for they proposed to arrive at the river 11 miles upstream from where Tom and the river team were counting on our resupply and support to get out. We had received no location or progress report from Tom for the last two days, and if he and the river team passed unwittingly before we descended to the river, the outcome could be serious indeed. From the map and satellite images it seemed much more promising to try to work eastward to Rainbow Falls by staying high on the ridge than by trying to follow the river bottom on foot. And the sullen attitude of the Monpas made it seem unlikely that we could coax them into climbing back for a second try if once we descended and stalled.

I hauled the satellite maps from their waterproof envelope in the top flap of my backpack, spread them over an ice-planed boulder in correct orientation to the terrain, and indicated emphatically where Rainbow Falls lay and how much hinged on our arrival there. Now with an eagle's, if not a satellite's, view ourselves, perhaps our intention was clearer than it had been in the abstract back in Mendung. Or perhaps my tone of voice made it clear that neither gasping for breath on every step nor slipping and falling on every other one would convince us to settle for an easier goal. The three Monpas and Ang Kami returned to the anxiously watching group, and an animated discussion ensued; Dave and I, with Lobsang, refolded our maps with feigned unconcern.

Covertly watching body language and eavesdropping on voice tones, Dave concluded that Squad Leader was speaking up, in his erratic and demonstrative way, for going onward. Several others were clearly reluctant, and Peme Gompa was completely unreadable. After about 15 minutes, Ang Kami returned to report that they had decided, "if Wick and Dave can go on, they will try it."

Eager to get out of the chill wind and warm up our stiff muscles, we all hastily shrugged into our packs and dropped down the gully on the southern side of the pass, Dave and I soberly considering the abrupt collective transformation that had occurred above. To neither of us did it feel like a malicious and premeditated conspiracy, although of course the Monpas had all known we would reach this end of their territory. It had more the flavor of a sullen aggression springing from insecurities that they were only themselves beginning to feel as they crossed into the unknown.

To underestimate the gulf that separated our perspectives would not be wise. The Monpas were surefooted and intimately familiar with every memorized inch of their rugged territory, yet they feared the unknown that stalked beyond the firelight of their ancestral knowledge. Since childhood, we confidently and sometimes rashly leaped around the globe, trusting the abstract knowledge of maps and written descriptions and scientific deduction. That unknown, which we firmly intended to explore, consisted of some of the most forbidding physical terrain on Earth, and perhaps it was an equally daunting metaphysical landscape for the Monpas. Clearly there was unfinished business.

ABOUT 500 VERTICAL FEET BELOW THE LIP, the tracing of a trail crossed our downward route, traversing the mountainside both east and west. That it was heavily used by cloven takin hooves was obvious; whether it was more than a meandering game trail was uncertain. In any case it would be the beginning of our route in the morning.

CHAPTER 9

TRAGEDY

The mountains lay, stood,
reared like creatures that dream lovely
in sunlight: ebony, silver and silk just as before.
But I loathed them,
trembling and sick, for you had gone.[1]

—WILFRID NOYCE

 HE FOLLOWING EXCHANGES ARE from the communications records of Harry Wetherbee, beginning 1900 hours, October 16, 1998:

TOM: *"Harry, this is Tom. Harry, we… had a very upsetting development here today, and that is—brace yourself for this—Doug was swept downriver into a huge rapid…and I'm really expecting the worst. Over."*

HARRY: *"…Oh boy…. Have you got your location? Over."*

TOM: *"We are about two hundred yards downstream of our location last night, and this occurred about 1130 this morning. Over."*

HARRY: *"OK, ...is there anything we can..."*

TOM: *"I don't know quite how to handle this, but I think the first thing to do is to alert Wick and see what he says about what we should do in terms of notifying the authorities and such—he might have some good advice about it. Over."*

HARRY: *"OK. ...maybe we can get a search party down from Mendung or Zhachu. Over."*

TOM: *"That could be...get a search party on the river? He was last seen being swept through some very big rapids. We hiked downstream about 2 1/2 – 3 miles and saw no sign of him. Over."*

HARRY: *"OK, what I will do is try to get hold of Wick. In fact my time with Wick is 1930; maybe you better call him directly. Perhaps he can get someone back to Mendung and Zhachu and get a search party out there. Over."*

TOM: *"All right, then, I will try him at 7:30... I don't know how this should be handled, how much we want it spread around until we really know what happened and we know what we want to say to the public. Over."*

HARRY: *"That's up to Wick to decide.... I don't think we can get there from here. I would say the only thing is to keep hiking down in that area and we'll try to get someone down the other way. Over."*

TOM: *"The river is moving at tremendous speed—it's just hard to say where he might be but...we haven't really discussed what we want to do next. We went down pretty far...."*

HARRY: *"Hello. Hello. Was he out of his boat? Over."*

TOM: *"No, the last we saw him, he was in his boat, upside down, and he was in a very, very big rapid and he just disappeared—his boat and he just disappeared— Like I said, we went quite a distance. There was some quiet water below, but there was no sign of him. So, I'm expecting the worst."*

HARRY: *"OK."*

TOM: *"When can I contact you again? Where are you now? Over."*

HARRY: *"We're on the road. We were about 3 or 4 hours back on the road; we were heading toward Trulung.... Let's see...Why don't you call me back after you talk to Wick, or have Wick call me? So I will stand by after your 7:30 phone call—how's that?—for further instructions. Over."*

TOM: *"OK, I'll do that. I'll recontact you, or ask Wick to call. Say 8 o'clock. Over."*

HARRY: *"OK, I will be standing by. And if there is anything we can do, we will certainly do it. Over."*

TOM: *"OK, Harry, thank you. Tom out."*

HARRY: *"Harry out."*

Our brief and tenuous satellite-telephone links were now vital. Each of the three widely separated teams had to be immediately redirected, and they had to plan and execute a mutually supporting search and rescue. Because of our limited and unpredictable battery power, Tom and I were restricted to terse, essential calls on a rigid schedule, even in this emergency. As a result of using radio language to ensure brevity and clarity, and to avoid the confusion sometimes created by the time delay of the signal relaying through the satellite far above our heads, our voices had the deliberately laconic ring of air-traffic controllers dealing with an emergency, or of military commanders in battle. These brief, detached-sounding exchanges were nevertheless a heartening touch of support and companionship among our small isolated groups as the shock of the loss, grief, and physical stress mounted.

1930 hours, October 16, 1998:

WICK: *"Harry, this is Wick. Do you have anything before I give you my situation report? Over."*

HARRY: *"Yes, Tom is trying to get you...Doug was swept downriver this morning about one one three zero hours. They are about 200 yards from where they were last night. They hiked down several miles, past big rapids, were unable to find him. The river is at a tremendous speed there, he said. The boat was upside down and he disappeared into the rapids. He was going to try to call you to discuss what might be done. Over."*

WICK: *"...Roger... From here, I can't imagine anyone but our two teams who could do anything constructive.... And until we know exactly what is going on, let's have no communication about this outside—at least until Tom and I can talk. Over."*

HARRY: *"No, I agree. He was going to try to call you at 7:30. Over."*

WICK: *"He was going to initiate the call? Is that correct? Over."*

HARRY: *"Correct."*

WICK: *"OK. I'll stand by for the next half hour.*

Over."

HARRY: "All right, let me try to call him and get him in touch with you. Over."

WICK: "Anything further at this time? Over."

HARRY: "Can you give me your location? Over."

WICK: "Roger. Two niner four six point eight six seven north. Zero niner five zero three point six seven four east. How copy? And give me your location and status. Over."

HARRY: "OK. We started our drive back from Pei toward Truʔung today. I'm not sure what we could do. Call me if you think there's anything we could do. I think it would be about ten days before we could get anyone up into that area. Maybe a little bit less if they went fast. But let me get off. I will call Tom and try to get him in contact with you, and after you talk please contact me and give me further instructions. Over."

WICK: "Roger. Please stand by for a follow-up after my call from Tom. Say at eight o'clock? Over."

HARRY: "I will be standing by from eight o'clock. I will stand by from eight to eight fifteen. Harry out."

WICK: "Wick out."

1940 hours on October 16, 1998:

HARRY: "This is Harry. Go ahead. Over."

TOM: "This is Tom, Harry. I had no luck contacting Wick. Over."

HARRY: "OK. I was in contact with Wick and he was waiting for your call....I've been trying to get you, and the switch says that I can't get you, so there's some-

thing wrong…I can get back with Wick and try to have him call you. Over."

TOM: *"OK. I'll stand by. I'll leave the phone on and if it rings I'll pick it up. Over."*

HARRY: *"OK. I also will leave the phone on standby all night, in case you need anything. How are your batteries holding out? Over."*

TOM: *"I have one good one…and this one looks good as well. So, I have one I haven't used yet. Over."*

HARRY: *"OK. I have been having trouble getting you. You seem to be able to get me. I will try to call Wick and have him keep trying. How long will you be on standby? Over."*

TOM: *"I'll be on standby until—shall we say until eight thirty?"*

HARRY: *"OK. I will try to pass that to Wick that you'll be on standby until eight thirty. Over."*

TOM: *"OK. Tom out."*

HARRY: *"Harry out."*

Maddening, seemingly capricious glitches in dialing kept Tom and me from making direct contact, but fortunately we were both able to maintain links to Harry. This vital relay allowed us to cobble together a swift, coordinated search involving the three separate teams.

2000 hours, October 16, 1998:

WICK: *"Hello. This is Wick. Over."*

HARRY: *"Wick, this is Harry. I just talked to Tom again. He is unable to get in contact with you. He is unable to get in contact with you. Do you want to give him a try? Over."*

WICK: *"I just did, and I got "insufficient digits," so I am unable to do it from this end.... Let me give you some directions to relay to Tom if you are able to contact him. Are you ready to copy? Over."*

HARRY: *"Ready to copy. Over."*

WICK: *"OK In the morning we will proceed on the left bank from our present location overlooking Pemakochung to Tom's reported location. We will attempt walkie-talkie commo the first five...hour."*

HARRY: *"Break. Break. I lost a couple of words there. You are going to attempt walkie-talkie contact at what time? Over."*

WICK: *"We will attempt walkie-talkie contact the first five minutes of every daylight hour. How copy? Over."*

HARRY: *"Got that fine. I will do my best to pass that on. I can give you Tom's last location—last coordinates. Are you ready to copy? Over."*

WICK: *"Ready to copy. Over."*

HARRY: *"OK. These are from a couple of days ago, but I believe they are in this general vicinity: two niner four five point four two—niner four five seven point niner five. Over."*

WICK: *"Roger. Good copy. Further instructions: We will be here standing by for Inmarsat commo at oh eight hundred in the morning and nineteen hundred in the evening. How copy? Over."*

HARRY: *"I copied that fine. I am going to try to leave my Inmarsat on standby throughout the night...wait one...I will leave my Inmarsat on standby throughout the night in case anybody needs me. Over."*

WICK: *"Roger. I would like you to find a good camp-site and just hold fast where you are and act as a commo base. Do you have vehicle battery power so you are able to do standby monitoring? Over."*

HARRY: *"Yes. We are with the truck. We have good batteries. We will stand by here and monitor the Inmarsat as best we can at all times. Over."*

WICK: *"OK, roger. Do the best you can, but prior-ity to the first ten minutes of every hour. That is the time that we will try to do our commo. Over."*

HARRY: *"All right. I understand that you will try to do the first ten minutes of every hour, although I will try to monitor twenty-four hours a day. Over."*

WICK: *"Roger. Nothing further here. I am going to break down commo and will not be back up until 0800 tomorrow morning. Anything further for me? Over."*

HARRY: *"Negative. I'll try to pass this on to Tom. Harry out."*

WICK: *"Wick out."*

0830 hours, October 17, 1998:

HARRY: *"This is Harry. Go ahead. Over."*

TOM: *"This is Tom, Harry. Did you get through to Wick? Over."*

HARRY: *"OK, Tom. Yes, I did get a message. I talked to Wick last night and just now. He is directly above Pemakochung, and he is right now descending to the river on river left in the vicinity*

*of Pemakochung and will work his way upriver
on river left to rendezvous with you. What bank are you
on? Over."*

TOM: *"Harry we're on the left bank now. We are
going to cross to the right and go downstream. There's a
place just upstream from Pemakochung marked on the
map as a lake. It won't really be a lake, but we should
be able to cross back to the left there. Over."*

HARRY: *"OK. Wick has the walkie-talkie, and he
will attempt walkie-talkie contact the first five minutes
of every daylight hour. Over."*

TOM: *"OK, I understand, but we will not be anywhere close enough for contact for at least a day. Could
you let Wick know that? Over."*

HARRY: *"I think it's too late. I think he has packed
up and he will be attempting to contact you. You might
just listen. Also he will be standing by on Inmarsat at
eight a.m., eight a.m., and at seven p.m., seven p.m. for
contact from you I know you are having trouble connecting. I am going to talk to Beijing Marine today and
see if I can get that straightened out. Over."*

TOM: *"OK, I'll try to call tonight. Tom out."*

HARRY: *"OK, good luck. Harry out."*

These short, remote exchanges colored our individual responses
to the emergency in incongruous ways. We were able to accomplish all necessary coordination, but the terse messages and the
necessity to relay everything through Harry led to three different perspectives and emotional responses throughout the early
days of the search.

FROM THE FLAT-TOPPED BOULDER where I perched on the morning of October 17 and learned via the Inmarsat telephone that Harry, 35 miles upstream at Pei, had no update to the evening's shocking news of Doug's accident, I could see directly down a wide, V-shaped ravine. The Tsangpo traced a smooth curve below, its white rapids and gray-green flow contained between rocky banks. To the right, our horizon was formed by a long rocky ridge plunging south from Gyala Pelri, forcing the river to detour around its nose. Beyond, not eight miles distant, I knew Tom, Jamie, and Roger were forcing their way downstream, hoping to meet Doug around every rock—if they had not found him already.

As soon as the phone call was over, we hastily packed up camp and began the descent, our sense of urgency heightened by the night's enforced delay. Although the river seemed just below our feet, it was actually seven hours of difficult climbing away, seven hours in which to rehearse in my mind what might be the outcome below.

The possibility of Doug's death in the Tsangpo was undeniable. This was a risk we dealt with in our sport and discussed openly. As Jamie had recently written, *...the stark accident numbers include more than a few friends....* [2] Doug had himself written just a year previously of the river death of Rich Weiss, a close friend and two-time Olympian:

> *For many top paddlers, racers and cruisers alike, it has been all too easy to ignore the increasing number of river deaths. "That wouldn't have happened to me...I'm better than he was...I'm smarter than that," are the subconscious thoughts which many, including myself, have had.*

Sorry, folks, but that won't cut it any longer.
They don't come any better or any smarter than Rich
Weiss. It's time to say it out loud: paddling Class VI white
water (and yes, that's what it should be called despite
the prevalent attitude here in the West) is risky business.
Will I still teach my son to paddle? Absolutely, and I
wager Rich would have also. The joy, the satisfaction,
the personal growth I've experienced through paddling
and the spectacular places I've seen are well worth the
risk. But let's not pretend that the risk isn't there. It's
there and it's very real and if we don't do everything we
can to deal with it and minimize it, then we've missed a
very important lesson. [3]

I was still a long way from considering a fatal outcome proba-
ble, however, from the few facts that I had received through
Harry: *"...Doug was swept downriver this morning...the boat was*
upside down and he disappeared into the rapids...." My enormous
and justified faith in Doug's competence on the water and in
the protection of his full dry suit, life jacket, and helmet reinforced the natural reaction of denial. Despite a number of cau-
tionary experiences, none of us on this expedition had ever, in
more than a cumulative century of river running, actually experienced a river death within our party, neither on expedition
nor on weekend excursions. Regardless of what we wrote, discussed, or told ourselves, deep down in our experience and
emotions drowning did always happen to "the other guy."

With considerable hope and escalating urgency, we therefore plunged down the hillside to join in the search for our missing man or to get Dave on the scene if—as was more

likely—Tom, Jamie, and Roger had already located Doug, and he was injured.

Our route ran initially down the moss-and-lichen-covered rubble at the base of the ravine, an irregular staircase used before us by the takin, goral (a reddish, goatlike antelope first "collected" for Western natural science by F.M. Bailey[4]), and at least one bear. As this chute became steeper, we were forced onto the flanking ridge, each change of route maddeningly forcing us to the left, farther downstream and away from the scene of the search. The vegetation thickened and changed, until soon we were descending beneath gigantic rhododendron trees, trunks two feet across and ropy twisted branches forming a solid canopy overhead, easy walking on an almost barren, parklike floor. We took full advantage of the swift going, almost oblivious in our concern and haste to one of the most spectacular old-growth forests on Earth.

When we took a midday tea and lunch stop, the Monpas were hard to read, talking quietly among themselves and offering little for Ang Kami's translation. How much they understood or cared about the emergency unfolding below was unclear. Dave and I speculated on whether they were silent in sympathy with our own somber mood. Or perhaps they had interpreted the outcome of the previous afternoon's confrontation about the route as a victory for the least cooperative faction? We had reversed ourselves almost immediately and opted for the route they had initially insisted upon.

We dropped off the nose of the rhododendron-covered ridge we had been following into another steep gully, again to the left, yet farther downstream. At one awkward, 200-foot section of muddy, steep rock, we set a series of ropes for handholds and lowered the backpacks from a belay around a tree. What had been a distant rumble from the river that morning had steadily increased in volume, and glimpses through the vegetation showed the far shore becoming closer. In mid-afternoon we finally broke from the forest, over a muddy five-foot embankment onto the hundred-foot-wide strip of bare, water-rounded boulders forming the Tsangpo's left bank. Turning right, we began to work our way upstream, eyes eagerly trained on both shores; we were finally part of the search, roughly 27 hours after Doug had last been seen.

A FEW HUNDRED YARDS UPSTREAM LAY THE FIRST RAPID—a big, booming chute in the center of the river—its explosive waves intermittently throwing spray 20 feet into the air. From what passed as a pool below, waves three feet high rolled in like surf to a rock-and-gravel beach, and overlooking the pool perched a gigantic boulder, slab sides 30 feet high, deeply undercut with sand-floored grottoes tunneled beneath. The scattered bones of a goral and clawed, hand-size pugmarks tracking the white sand beneath the rock indicated we were not the first to discover this spacious lair. This comfortable but slightly surreal place we dubbed "Panther Beach"—although the former inhabitant was probably actually a golden leopard—and asserted squatters' rights.

Reconnaissance upstream revealed a small cliff dropping directly into the river a half mile above Panther Beach, cutting off progress up the shoreline and dictating a base camp at the huge boulder. And here the Monpas dug in. To my mounting frustration and anger, and Ang Kami's, they announced that this was the end of the line because there were no trails; to go on, they demanded double wages. Before I could respond to this baldly mercenary attempt to take advantage of our desperate search for Doug, Dave stepped forward from the background and, from the depths of a nearly forgotten course on hostage negotiations, counseled immediately adjourning the discussion rather than trying to make decisions in the middle of this shouting, trilingual caucus. Perhaps in the morning the Monpas could come to us with their ideas on what we all could and should do.

OVERRIDING MY NATURAL REACTION TO THIS COERCION had to be two paramount goals: pursuing the search for Doug with the utmost speed and thoroughness, and then getting our entire group out of the gorge safely, perhaps with an injured man. Capitulation to escalating demands was not necessarily wise, nor was going it alone. Without explaining himself specifically, Ang Kami advised against offering too much pay, although he did not rule out some increase. Interestingly, he also advised against offering a reward for search results in lieu of increased pay.

From the map and satellite images we could tell we were in an excellent position for the search, eight miles downstream from the accident site, with Tom, Jamie, and Roger sweeping down and ourselves sweeping up. While I was still optimistic that Doug might be found alive, I also knew that such a fortunate event would almost have to occur in the first mile or two below the accident area. No matter how well protected, no swimmer or out-of-control boater could realistically survive the Tsangpo longer than that. Even if Doug had regained control after he was last seen and had paddled or washed downriver to find a take-out spot, he would never have gone beyond the flat stretch of river a mile upstream from Panther Beach. Anything we found downstream would be bad news, while the odds would become more promising every step we took upstream. By the time the teams linked up we would have covered every yard where Doug could be alive.

Morning did bring cooler heads and more constructive suggestions, and my principles against being coerced did allow for an effort to divide and conquer. A small, light, and fast party of three Monpas and Ang Kami would find a way above the water-level cliffs and search upstream, ideally making contact with Tom and returning to base after two days. For their willingness and the extra difficulties they would face, these three would indeed receive increased wages. Happily, the three toughest woodsmen—Peme Gompa, Squad Leader, and Redford—were also the three who seemed most loyal to us, and I did not resent paying a bonus to them.

To each man we issued a supply of freeze-dried food, and I gave Ang Kami my bivvy sack because good campsites were unlikely. The four trudged off into the forest behind Panther Beach immediately after lunch, all three Monpas with rifles loaded at the ready. On their own initiative, Lobsang and Chaplain soon headed downstream to search for evidence of the accident, while the rest of the Monpas drifted off to hunt.

For Dave and me, waiting for news at the base camp rather than heading upstream to join the search was frustrating. Realistically, however, the four we had sent would travel much faster, and with keener eyes, than we could ourselves. And in Ang Kami and Peme Gompa I had absolute faith; they would do everything that could be done. We could do little, except call hourly on the walkie-talkie in the hope of raising Tom—

or better yet, of course, Doug, who had also been carrying a walkie-talkie when he was lost. Dave recorded in his journal: *Next contact time is nineteen hundred hours, and our hopes are becoming prayers.*

The sole luxury item Dave had brought in his rucksack was a dog-eared copy of Charles Frazier's Civil War novel *Cold Mountain*. This I now borrowed and began to read cover to cover, compulsively escaping from the roar of the river, my constant worry about Doug, and my anger at the Monpas. I found refuge in a different century, a different continent, even a different identity.

Camped in a rocky field of sparse grass and yak dung beside the unpaved "highway" to Pei were Harry, Doris, and Paulo, who were denied even the catharsis of physical effort. Theirs was a vital link, of course, for if Tom or I lost contact, or we otherwise could not find each other, both the search effort and the safety of all concerned would be in jeopardy. When the time came for contact with families, government officials, and the outside world, they would become a busier communications hub. Meanwhile, there was little to do except relay messages twice a day, monitor the otherwise silent telephone for emergencies, and ponder Tom's ominous initial report: "...I'm really expecting the worst."

Small groups of children drifted through the camp at all hours, many bound to and from a collective school not far away, others herding sheep and goats, all quick to poke their heads unbidden into any open tent fly or vehicle, as uninhibited as all Tibetans about freely examining every item of equipment. What had been cute and local color earlier in the trip was now constant irritant, invading the space and distracting the attention of the three increasingly concerned Americans. Doris retreated into their large black-and-yellow tent, zipping closed the nylon doors even in the stifling midday heat to exclude the constantly peering faces. Just as I was escaping into the novel *Cold Mountain* at Panther Beach, she plowed nonstop through the melodramatic *Beach Music*, retreating through Fat Conroy's vivid descriptions back to the Rome of the 1960's where Doris had lived and gone to school.

Downstream from the accident site, Tom, Roger, and Jamie searched with mounting shock and grief, without the hope Dave and I still clung to.

THE MORNING OF OCTOBER 16 HAD STARTED WELL, without premonition, a day of blue skies and brilliant white cumulus clouds. Tom led initially, picking routes down the left shore through chutes and drops that could be scouted from his boat. At a small ledge above the first major rapid, the four paddlers stopped to scout from shore and discussed possible lines to run the ledge before carrying the rapid downstream. As was typical, Doug elected to run first and walked back up the shore to his boat, continuing to study the routes, while Tom worked his way to a rocky vantage point below with throw rope and video camera.

Doug swung wide from the shore, then angled back to the left, accelerating his boat toward the choice of possible routes farthest from shore. There the water poured nearly vertically over the lip in a chute about 8 feet high and 15 feet wide, forming a deep recirculating hole at its base with most of the current flowing out of the right corner. As the group had discussed while scouting, running the left corner of this chute and just clipping the left edge of the hole below seemed to be the straightest, cleanest line available; the significant disadvantage was that if the boat failed to clear the recirculating hole, it, or a swimmer, would probably flush out to the right, into current leading directly to the massive rapid downstream.

That "worst case" was exactly what Tom saw unfold through his viewfinder. Doug flew across the corner of the lip in good position, paddling hard to maintain momentum and leaning back to keep the boat level and propelled downstream. For a brief second the landing also looked fine, until the momentum slowed, then ceased. Inch by inch the boat was drawn back to the recirculating water at the base of the chute. When the stern plunged into the downward power of the chute, the boat was flipped violently end-over-end, and for 16 thrashing seconds it tumbled, trapped between falling water and backwash.

With relief, Tom saw the boat flush out the right-hand corner of the hole and begin to drift slowly downstream with Doug still in it; surely now he would roll up and paddle swiftly to the safety of the shoreline, as he had seen him do hundreds of times before after somewhat similar mishaps. This time, however, Tom's relief turned to horror. Doug's first—and then second—uncharacteristically labored efforts to roll failed halfway up, and the capsized boat accelerated into the maw of the first big hole 200 yards downstream, a green-and-white trench 40 yards long and 10 to 20 feet deep athwart the centerline of the current.

Snatching up only his yellow throw rope and belting it around his waist like a fanny pack, Tom chased desperately on foot over the shoreline boulder field. Like slow-motion flight in a nightmare, his every effort to run was thwarted by the tumbled, slippery rocks. In minutes that seemed like hours he arrived panting at the base of the rapid, and Tom felt cold despair replace adrenaline. The first big hole where he had last seen Doug was but the first of six in the length of the rapid, and the power in any of them would be virtually impossible to survive.

ABOVE, ROGER REMAINED TRANSFIXED. In the midst of his horror a calm, cold voice in his mind told him to keep his eye on Doug as long as possible and to memorize every detail for clues that might later guide the search. For long, awful moments he watched as Doug and his kayak, in the middle of a third Eskimo roll attempt, fell into the first gaping hole and disappeared from sight. A flash of color appeared tumbling into the next hole downstream, too far away for Roger to tell if there was an occupant, and again disappeared; it reappeared briefly for the last time in the third hole At last convinced that he would see no more, Roger raced after Tom.

They saw no sign of Doug or his equipment in the surging pool below the rapid, so Tom and Roger continued their urgent search downstream, shouting and blowing the whistles they each carried attached to the zippers of their life jackets for this purpose, hoping against hope for a response. "As we came around every boulder, we hoped to hear Doug say, 'Hey, guys,' but of course we knew it wasn't going to happen," Tom would later recall. All they heard was the ominous thunder of the river.

FROM FARTHER UPSTREAM, WHERE THE BOATS WERE PULLED out on shore, Jamie saw the tragedy unfold. Hastily ripping the drybags of gear and food from his boat, he hoisted the lightened

craft to his shoulder and, using his paddle as a walking stick, followed Tom and Roger as best he could. Speed was vital, but so
might be the mobility of a boat.

For the next several days of shock and dawn-to-dark searching, the daily journals of the river team remained blank. Jamie
later recalled the first frantic 24 hours:

> I had paddled down the tail of the rapid where Doug
> had died, across a large uneasily churning pool, and
> then down a wide, wide rapid where I threaded between
> large holes, reading where to go in quick glances from
> the tops of waves. I made it to the left bank, feeling that
> I had just taken too great a risk, and swearing that I
> wouldn't do that again.
>
> I continued down the left side, through a rock gar-
> den visited by a surf of rogue waves coming from the main
> current, until I met Tom and Roger, just downstream of
> the large glacier that had pushed ice and dirty gravel down
> to the riverside. They scouted ahead for me, told me to stay
> left, which I did, passing them; they continued to work
> their way down the left bank. I had to get out and scout
> twice, kept running down the left side, handling the drops
> fine but feeling frightened and oppressed the whole time.
> They re-passed me in this section; we exchanged a few
> more sentences.
>
> Soon the rapids got more and more difficult, the side
> channels I was using funneled back into the river, and I
> dared go no farther. I pulled out and lay down on a flat
> slab of rock, resting, waiting for Tom and Roger to return
> from downstream.
>
> After a time I began to wonder why they had not

returned. They could not go very far; downstream a high rocky ridge blocked the left bank, ending in a vertical cliff that dropped, sheer and wet with spray, into the muscular currents of the river. Leaving my boat propped vertically, so they could not miss it, I rose and set off downstream looking for Roger and Tom.

I picked my way down over and between a collection of large to enormous rocks, sometimes taking to the brambles on one side, then coming back to the rocks again. As I approached the cliff, the bank became steeper, until I was climbing, clinging to trees, slithering down steep gullies, sidling along rocky ledges. Finally I was unwilling to go on, yet had still not seen Tom and Roger.

I tried to retrace my path, but could not remember how I had come. When I finally reached my boat again I found a rough arrow of driftwood and stones, pointing upriver. They had been there, and gone on.

As I had unloaded my food and gear at the very beginning of my rescue attempt, I had little choice but to follow. The sun was just setting, and though it felt very strange to do so, I took some photos of the glacier upstream, with the sun shining in from one side, through the gorge. The world seemed to have picked up the feelings inside me, and was painting them across the enormous landscape with majestic and unearthly light, a light like the sound of violins, mountains like drums, river like horns and cymbals and trumpets.

Leaving my boat, I trudged and clambered back the way I had paddled. Slowly, step by step, in the huge aloneness, I waded the glacier-cold stream. I crossed mud *and gravel. I moved on into undergrowth threaded with low takin trails. I climbed up and down small cliffs to search out a better route.*

I was just opposite the whirlpool-infested pool when I heard Doug's voice shout "Jamie!"

The breath went out of me. I forced my way out of the bushes to the edge of a 15-foot escarpment and looked down on the rocks lining the river below me. The water was flowing upstream, in a large circular eddymoving up as fast as most rivers ever flow down. There were eddies within this eddy, formed by irregularities in the bank. Breathing hard, I looked up and down. No one.

I moved back and forth around the bushes, for a better view. Finally I found a way down the escarpment, and searched among the rocks. Nothing.

I listened. The river was making a number of distinct sounds. Hissing along the rocks. Slurping on the eddy line. Plopping and clopping farther out. A chorus, from upstream and down, of rolling churning roars that came from a host of recirculating holes and endlessly breaking waves. Thumps as uprearing waves fell back upon themselves. Surf against the shoreline rocks. Out of these sounds I could almost hear human sounds form: incoherent shouts, mutterings, a babble of proto-voices. These must have fooled me. I searched a while longer,and then gave up, reclimbed the bank, and made my way upstream.

It was after dark when I finally reached the place where Doug had been swept away. Up on the steep hill beside me a small light showed. I shouted, but they did not hear me. Wearily I climbed up and joined them on an uneven flattening in the hillside. A fire burned. Water was hot. We commiserated. We cried a little. We ate and drank.

That night the stars came out, for the first time in a week.

During the next days of riverside hiking, and occasional paddling, I heard more voices, though never Doug's again. I heard a chorus of children singing; snatches of conversation; shouts and exclamations, all formed from the chaos of surging water sounds, and melding back into river sounds again. It was eerie, startling, and oddly comforting. A reminder that all of civilized life was still going on somewhere, waiting for our return.

For the next three days, as shock, grief and physical exhaustion built for all three paddlers, Roger took more of the initiative. He found routes, built rock cairns to keep track of where they had been, set the pace, and selected camps. After retrieving Jamie's boat from downstream and the other two from above, they crossed below the accident site. Leaving the boats at the crossing point, they searched down the right shore on foot, just as they had on the left the previous day, but this time they carried food and bivouac gear.

AT JUST AFTER 4:00 P.M. ON THE AFTERNOON OF OCTOBER 18, 52 hours after Doug was last seen, Dave heard a sudden break in the static hiss on the walkie-talkie he was monitoring, and a single, unintelligible word, but nothing further. Eagerly we hustled up the shoreline boulders to the cliffs a half mile upstream, and from there at exactly 5:00 p.m. Tom's weary voice was plain, even over the river's incessant interference. He, Jamie, and Roger were on the far shore, a quarter mile upstream, at the brief flat interval on the river we had selected as the rendezvous point. Tom could see Ang Kami and Peme Gompa across the river. By sight and voice, if not yet touching, the teams were linked up.

Tom's sober, disillusioning account of Doug's accident, together with the fact that search parties had now covered the full length of the river for more than 11 miles downstream without result, dictated that this was the turning point we had hoped and prayed to avoid. Our friend and teammate had perished; further efforts would not result in rescue.

We would continue searching for his body and his equipment, and the three paddlers needed to retrieve their boats from where they had left them upstream before they could cross the river and join us at the base camp. But now we must direct our plans and efforts to the difficult future: the dreadful task of notifying Doug's wife, Connie; reporting the incident to appropriate Chinese and American officials; dealing with the media. We had held the outside world at bay to concentrate on rescue as long as the smallest hope remained.

The first and most difficult duty fell upon Jamie, closest of us not only to Doug but also to his wife Connie in Salt Lake City. Immediately after Tom and I concluded our first radio conference, Jamie set up the satellite telephone and, through his wife Sandra, set the process in motion for Connie's visiting sister to inform her in person. Jamie then followed up the next day with a brief, awkward call directly to Connie. As much as he had steeled himself for the call, mentally rehearsing all pos-

sible thoughts, emotions, and words, he was totally unprepared
for the shock of Doug's voice on the answering machine before
Connie picked up.

CHAPTER 10

Uɴɪᴛᴇᴅ

*My final prayer was one of thanksgiving for a world filled with
the sublimity of the high places, for the sheer beauty of
the mountains and for the surpassing miracle that we should be
so formed as to respond with ecstasy to such beauty,
and for the constant element of danger without which the
mountain experience would not exercise such a grip on our
sensibilities. We then laid the body to rest in its icy tomb, at rest
on the breast of the Bliss-Giving Goddess Nanda.* [1]

—Wɪʟʟɪ Uɴsᴏᴇʟᴅ,
burying his daughter on Nanda Devi

WHEN THE TEAMS finally joined beneath the
looming, undercut boulder at Panther
Beach, emotional and physical reactions
battered us for two full days as if they were
waves breaking over our heads, then sucking at our feet upon
receding. We felt relief and comfort from unification of the two
small groups, grief over the loss of Doug, anger at the Monpas'
attempt to take advantage of us, and regret for the end of the
expedition and its tragic outcome.

Each of us was by now showing some physical reaction,
and Jamie's was the most severe. His frantic three-day search
down the river had been the most desperate, the loss of his closest friend the most staggering blow. Now, with hope abandoned

and his terrible duty to notify Connie Gordon discharged, his resistance collapsed after the days of adrenaline and tension. Roger helped him rig their tarpaulin over a sandy spot 30 feet away from the busy, communal camp under the rock, and he retreated into his bivvy bag with fever, nausea, and stomach cramps, emerging only to retch periodically. Dave made the rounds to check on everyone—American, Sherpa, and Monpa alike—seeing that Jamie took in plenty of fluids and treating infections on Roger's hands, boils on Ang Kami's back, leech bites on Peme Gompa's ankles. His quiet talk was more important than his medication.

Our first evening together at the base camp, Tom and I both looked regretfully downstream where the nose of a great glacier from Namcha Barwa emerged from the mist and almost reached the swift and relatively flat river, but we gave no serious thought to continuing the river exploration. There were practical considerations, of course. Jamie was ill, the Monpas teetered on the brink of rebellion, and Chinese authorities had to be notified of the incident. Those obstacles might have been overcome by sheer willpower, but in fact Doug had himself made the decision in advance, in his incisive fashion; he had done it during a difficult, necessary team discussion in a quiet corner of the spacious garden at our hotel in Kathmandu.

On September 25, 1998, Paulo Castillo made an audio/ video recording in which the following exchange occurred:

WICK: *"...But I do think we need to consider, and maybe have some group consensus on, what is the...abort moment, what...happens if things go badly wrong.... I've never been on a river trip where there was* a death, but suppose that were to happen? That has happened to other people."

JAMIE: "Are you asking if we would keep going?"

WICK: "That's a very basic question. I mean, what are people's thoughts on that?"

TOM: "A death on the river? And just leave the person?"

WICK: "Um...when I was on these river trips...and doing other travel...Laura knows perfectly well if she's ever asked that.. I don't want any bodies brought back or anything...carve my name on a tree and drive on. That's my own personal philosophy, but—I kind of hate to raise this, make people think of it—but I'd like to know, especially among you all, what your philosophy is, in advance."

DOUG: "...That's easy, at least for me. If I were the person to die, leave me there; and if someone dies, get to the nearest exit point."

WICK: "You think abort the expedition at that point and take out? Even if it could go on?"

DOUG: "I don't think I could go on."

WICK: "That's exactly the question I'm asking."

DOUG: "I just wouldn't—naa, I'd just feel like I ought to be home, talking to that person's family, doing something other than paddling whitewater, having fun."

WICK: "You're still thinking this is going to be fun?"

The others had been less specific, their ideas less well thought out, but with Doug's thoughts on the subject in mind, our direction was now clear: Get to the nearest exit point, get home, and do what we could for his family. He had also made it clear that he would choose for his body to be left in the river, so there was little point taking extra risk to extend the search beyond the limits where his survival was possible.

We also quietly reminded ourselves that it can sometimes be only a short step from a single tragedy, such as the one we were confronting, to the complete unraveling of the situation, where exhaustion, bad judgment, and letdown compound each other and multiple casualties result. We were in good control at the moment, united and resting up at Panther Beach, well supplied with food, and in communication with Harry at the nearest road. Yet none of the Americans were 100 percent healthy, the Monpas were unreliable, and we still had seven or so days of formidable terrain to cross. The risks and challenges were not over yet.

AFTER A DAY OF MUCH NEEDED REST, the following evening Tom led off our memorial to our friend with a Victorian-era gospel that reminded him of the early mountain mornings Doug had loved so well:

> *Morning has broken, like the first morning,*
> *Blackbird has spoken, like the first bird,*
> *Praise for the new day, praise for the morning,*
> *God's recreation of the first day.* [2]

Under a heavy mist condensing to light rain, in a solemn semi-circle we gathered near dusk facing the surging river: Jamie was pale but keeping to his feet, wrapped in an olive drab poncho I had been using as a ground sheet; Tom squinted wearily through rain-smeared glasses; Ang Kami and Lobsang were side by side, gazing thoughtfully down with their hands in their pockets; Roger stood in a bulky fleece jacket and ski cap between the gaunt McEwan brothers. The Monpas stood solemnly, rain glistening off their shiny black hair, hands together in the gesture of prayer and respect common to Christianity and Buddhism, the younger ones hanging back wide-eyed and perhaps a little fearful.

Tom looked up the immense valley, back toward where the accident had occurred, and intoned a short extemporaneous prayer, in Doug's memory but more for his wife Connie and their young sons, Tyler and Bryce. Then he turned and nodded to Chaplain, who, assisted by Squad Leader, continued the ceremony.

Aided by Lobsang they placed upright before the silent group a rectangular block of dark limestone about 14 inches high, upon which Tom had written out Doug's name in black ink. Two of the younger men hastened to the fire and returned to place smoldering brands beside the rock. A third fetched a bag of tsampa flour, which he sprinkled over the coals, producing a dense and pungent smoke. Taking from under their shirts the 108-bead Buddhist rosaries they wore like necklaces, Chaplain and Squad Leader began to repeat a mantra in a rhythmic chant that seemed to echo the backbeat of the river. The other Monpas began to drift back and forth, sometimes watching us and their chanting fellows, sometimes attending chores around the camp; they were clearly more relaxed now that our formal and unfamiliar rituals were completed.

When the chants tapered off and Chaplain indicated completion, Tom gestured for the young Monpas to return. In Tibetan they began to sing a melodic folk song. "Yarlung

Tsangpo," which was about the river and homeland and home-sickness. The semicircle broke up, ard all but one of its members returned to dry out by the campfires under the leaning walls of the huge rock. Lobsang picked up the limestone block with Doug's name and carried it down to the shore, carefully placing it as near as he could approach to the surging river to await the next summer flood. His back to the camp, he bowed his head and stood several long silent moments silhouetted against the bright exploding water.

The warmth and unity of the memorial service were unfortunately but an interval in an increasingly fractured relationship with the Monpas. The curiosity and natural friendliness of the youngest had if anything increased with the arrival of Tom, their hero of the year before. Management, however, in the form of Village Voice, had informed Ang Kami that morning that everyone now wanted a 70 percent increase in pay for the return journey.

This blatant attempt at extortion I immediately dismissed; Village Voice had badly miscalculated his timing and his understanding of Americans. Now that our isolated groups of two and three were together in a "critical mass," and particularly with Tom's iron will to back me up, there was no chance of our giving in. Furthermore, now that we had exhausted all chance of finding Doug alive, the overriding concern that had led me to raise the pay for the one search team no longer existed.

The following morning Village Voice returned to the subject with an ultimatum: Unless we agreed to higher rates, they would depart for Mendung without us. It was increasingly clear that he spoke from some position of authority and that the others, even Peme Gompa, were somehow constrained from challenging his decision even if they did not approve The limits of this authority and whether it sprang from election within the village, heredity, or appointment by the remote provincial government were unclear.

We were hardly helpless in this standoff. Although the route would be difficult to find unassisted in the incredibly convoluted terrain and dense vegetation, Ang Kami, Lobsang, Dave, and I had just traversed it, and Dave had recorded GPS coordinates at key landmarks. There would surely be numerous false starts, but with unflappable Ang Kami's sage advice and steadfast Lobsang's strength we would be able to find our way. Lobsang by now had revealed himself to be our steadiest and most loyal team member—the farthest thing from either "unemployable son-in-law" or "citified." His English, however, remained more optimistic than coherent. We had paid nothing of the wages earned so far; if the Monpas deserted, they would be forsaking the entirety of the biggest cash windfall Mendung village had seen in years. Finally, as I made ostentatiously clear each evening, we had the satellite telephone, over which I could call for outside assistance if absolutely necessary.

On the other hand, the still recovering paddlers were equipped only with river shoes and rucksacks designed to stow in boats, hardly ideal for carrying extra loads. The boats would be abandoned in any case, but we also had between $5,000 and $7,000 worth of boating and climbing gear, tents, and extra food that we would have to abandon if we walked out unassisted. And, as Roger dourly noted, the Monpas had all the guns.

Roger had once been robbed while someone held a machete to his throat in Jamaica, and on another occasion he had been abandoned on a wilderness road in the highlands of

Peru; thus, his informed perspective was sobering. Also, less than a year previously a college acquaintance of mine, Ned Gillette, had been murdered in the Gilgit Valley, up which the Wetherbees and I had traveled on our way to the Khunjerab Pass on our cross-China trip. Robbers had surrounded his tent in the night and poured gunfire through the nylon walls until he was dead and his wife severely wounded. Like paddling accidents, violent attacks do not only happen to "the other guy."

At no time, however, did the Monpas even hint at physical violence. Dave and I agreed that we felt none of the eerie chill we both associated with armed confrontations in other places, with other groups. F.M. Bailey had noted: "What astonished us both…was the degree of security which we felt, though we were carrying with us a considerable sum in money and were very lightly armed."[4] For the moment it seemed this speculation was more in our minds than theirs.

In addition to the anger and determination not to be coerced, which I shared with Tom, some secret (and perhaps unworthy) part of me almost hoped the desertion would take place. Bereft of the chance to explore downstream, our way out on foot might become a challenging and very traditional adventure in itself. The porters of Jesuit Fathers Ippolito Desideri and Emanoel Freyre struck for more money on the Zoji pass in Ladakh at the opposite end of the Himalaya in 1715, the first recorded porter strike in the Himalaya. Almost 300 years later, in 1993, somewhere just across the Tsangpo from Panther Beach, six of nine Monpa guides and porters deserted Everest climber David Breashears and photographer Gordon Wiltsie. With the significant exception of Sherpa territory near Everest in Nepal, the regularity of such incidents made the porter strike a "time-honored feature of all the best Himalayan expeditions," in the words of historian Charles Allen.[3]

At my side, my white-mustached conscience counseled that despite the relief of delicious righteous anger, and my secret urge to join the ranks of "all the best Himalayan expeditions," it was in everyone's best interest, Americans no less than Monpas, that we remain together.

Dave Phillips wrote in his journal on October 22, 1998:

> Ang Kami carefully dealt with this potentially explosive situation and the position from which Wick and Tom would not budge. The "Village Voice" is in a "win. lose" situation that costs both face and position should he not accomplish his aims [IF I ONLY HAD HIM ALONE IN WEST VIRGINIA FOR A FEW MINUTES]. He attempted a compromise by setting a new rate of 14 days at 80 Yuan (the original contract) and 8 additional days at 100 Yuan. I encouraged acceptance as a few additional Yuan would…get us out of a really bad spot, and also allow Village Voice to avoid a loss of face.
>
> Wick countered with 80 Yuan per day out-and-back as in the contract, but he wisely offered a 'carrot': a few more days of easy employment on the Po Tsangpo trail with additional Yuan in the new contract. "Village Voice" refused, saying other Mendung porters also needed employment and would carry on the Po Tsangpo route.
>
> Having reached the end of logical compromise, the entire porter crew packed and marched away—up into the forest—as we settled into place to plan our own march out of here alone, a tough walk even with porters and guides.

I wasn't yet overly concerned, believing this was simply a negotiating bluff on Village Voice's part. Earlier "Squad Leader" had caught my eye and gave me a quick smile and nod, and when no one could see us, "Redford" gripped both my hands and gave me a great smile of reassurance. These two are the strongest personalities in the group (outside of Peme Gompa and Village Voice) and both have reason to believe I saved their lives (possibly correct in the case of Redford). At no time did I feel we were in physical danger.

They left in single file, but after five minutes Squad Leader returned. He had no basket pack or rifle, but he had clearly stated to the rest of the Monpas that he would stay behind to help all of us find our way out of here. Within another five minutes other 'rebels' began to come in. "Point Man" stomped in—14 years old—and announced "Bad to the Bone" as others followed. We had five "rebel" porters with us; a group that included "Chaplain." We could now make it out of here in some degree of safety. Alone we could have made it, but it would have been a real trial!

Curiously, neither Peme Gompa nor Redford had returned. I wondered about this, but the mystery was solved as the rest of the "column" slowly marched back into camp. Peme Gompa came immediately to us and Redford came to me to grasp my hand again. Village Voice walked with his head down, looking dejected. He had clearly lost a major argument in the forest and the moderates were all with us once more.

The potential disaster of abandonment has been

avoided, but we are very cautious about showing our pleasure at this positive turn of events. No reason to push Village Voice into some additional reaction. It was good that we assumed a neutral—as neutral as possible—position with regard to the morning's problem. We essentially set the limits for the dialogue going on between Village Voice and his supporters and Peme Gompa and his troops. At no point did we get involved as the two factions deliberated.

The morning has been one of both high drama and suspense, but we have managed to survive it. Jamie is improving by the hour, and Tommy is back in his marvelous "Peter Pan" role with his "Lost Boys"—taping them and preparing to record songs on the digital video recorder. The Lost Boys love it, and this really serves us well as we attempt to casually increase the level of rapport we have with these young people.

What a day! And it's only noon.

In this uneasy partnership we spent the afternoon preparing loads for the exit march. The three paddlers slipped out of camp and quietly cached their boats in a deep ravine well above all high-water marks; we wanted neither floods nor teenage Monpa hands to launch them and create confusion if boat remnants were ever discovered downstream. The other boating gear was dried, folded, and disassembled for transport out. At the suggestion of Peme Gompa and Ang Kami, we willingly passed out freeze-dried dinners to supplement the Monpas' dwindling food supplies and lighten the loads a bit. Everything was set for a morning departure and the next phase of our journey.

As absorbed as we were in the strong currents swirling around our small group at Panther Beach, we could not ignore obligations to the world beyond as well. Now assured that Connie had been properly informed, our next urgent task was to notify Chinese authorities, the U. S. State Department, and our community of family, friends, expedition sponsors, and fellow paddlers at home, before rumor began.

Because we had recovered no body or physical evidence, it was of the utmost importance that our reports from the very beginning be absolutely accurate, absolutely consistent, and absolutely credible. Just as I had held out hope until I actually arrived on the scene and talked to the eyewitnesses, Doug's loved ones' first and powerful instincts probably would be to clutch at any straw, and their greater distance from the scene would magnify their uncertainty. In addition, Chinese law, like American, generally requires a waiting period before a missing person is declared dead; in practical terms such as insurance and legal status, it was equally important that our report be accepted as definitive enough to certify death. None of us beside the Tsangpo could have left the river if we had not been morally certain we had exhausted even the remotest possibility of finding our friend alive, but now we needed to communicate that certainty to others who had not been there.

Since even the slightest discrepancies or questions could have resulted in additional pain and difficulties, I had crafted a short but definitive statement, which I passed to Harry at 1900 hours on October 20 with instructions to begin the notifications:

It is our sad duty to report that on 16 October 1998 Douglas Gordon lost his life on the Tsangpo River in Tibet, vicinity 29 degrees 45 minutes North, 94 degrees 58 minutes East. Witnesses observed him swept into an almost certainly lethal set of rapids, from which he was not seen to emerge Five days of diligent search by members of his party, assisted by eleven Monpa hunters, failed to find Mr. Gordon or any of his equipment on either shore for a distance of approximately sixteen kilometers downstream.

Due to the nature of the river and surrounding terrain, his survival a greater distance than that is certainly impossible. Mr. Gordon is presumed to have died by drowning.

Elements of the search teams will assemble on 21 October and will begin trekking out of the Tsangpo Gorge via Mendung village and Peiung on the Lhasa-Chengdu highway. Estimated travel time is seven to ten days.

Those were the facts and the only details that were to be released until we got out of the gorge and had battery power to answer questions firsthand and in detail. Even then our amplification would be limited to whatever the Chinese authorities required of us, and to all the details we could provide in person to friends and families. All public information would be coordinated with the National Geographic Society.

THE SLOW WAIT AT THE WETHERBEE BASE CAMP beside the highway was now over. On the satellite telephone literally day and night because of time differences, Harry began three critical notifications.

The nearest U. S. State Department representation to Tibet was at the U. S. Consulate in Chengdu, and Harry telephoned them with our report, requesting that it be passed to the appropriate Chinese government officials. The Consul General in Chengdu could, if he received appropriate reports from Chinese investigators, execute the "Report of Death of a U. S. Citizen Abroad." By being aware of our situation from the beginning, and by seeing that the report and investigation were steered correctly through all the right Chinese channels, the consulate staff would be better able to head off problems and oversights in one of the largest bureaucracies on Earth.

Immediately after notifying the consulate, Harry called Jon Meisler—he had obtained our permits and coordinated our transport inside Tibet—at his family home in Pittsburgh, Pennsylvania. Jon, in turn, telephoned Lhasa and notified officers of the travel company supporting us, for it was vital that their reporting correspond with ours. Their representatives in the field with us had seen only parts of the situation as it unfolded at their various locations, and Harry and I had allowed no piecemeal reporting over the satellite telephones.

Lastly, Harry called Sarah Park, the "tenth member" of our expedition team, in Potomac, Maryland, and transformed her role from background to public forefront.

MONTHS BEFORE, I HAD ASKED SARAH, TOM'S SIGNIFICANT OTHER and business partner in their Calleva School of Paddling, if she would take on the role of our official representative and point of contact in the United States when we were in Tibet, and she had gamely agreed with barely a hesitation in her voice or a crack in her smile. Being left "flying a desk," passing periodic status reports to sponsors and perhaps coordinating an occasional live interview with National Public Radio, was in reality the last thing the slim, athletic sportswoman and equestrian trainer wanted. She had watched intently for two years as the expedition grew from long-shelved dream to reality. Raised in southern Africa, educated in England, and well-traveled around the globe, she heard the same drummer as the rest of us, understood the romance, felt the tug.

Now, as news of the tragedy inevitably began to break in the United States, questions needed to be fielded from concerned families and friends, involved sponsors, and hungry press. Personally focused on getting us out of the gorge, I was grateful for the combination of luck and loyalty that left these external matters in Sarah's independent hands. She had accompanied Tom on numerous boating trips to Mexico, Canada, and points between, and she understood white-water expeditions and how we ran them. Having followed the Tsangpo plans as they evolved, she had details at her fingertips. She also possessed a quiet firmness, an assurance of manner and voice forged in English public schools and honed at Saint John's College, Oxford. It would serve her, and us, well.

Sarah's initial steps were straightforward. She telephoned the families of each expedition member to ensure that everyone was informed of the situation and to assure them that no other team members were in danger. Next she notified points of contact at the American Canoe Association, the Explorers Club, and the National Geographic Society, who would use my statement as the basis for an October 20 press release. Lastly, she relayed the same statement to an e-mail list of 50 or so friends and sponsors of the expedition.

Within hours, however, her role was to become more complicated. News organizations, particularly the *Washington Post*, with its long tradition of covering D.C.-area white-water sport, picked up the story and pressed for details. And within the paddle-sport world every sort of speculation and rumor began to circulate by e-mail and chat room. In a sense more isolated and alone than we were at Panther Beach, Sarah manned the electronic ramparts and defended our privacy with steady salvos of "the only information available is what is in the statement" and "don't believe the rumors; wait until they return."

CHAPTER 11

EXIT

This has been a chapter of disasters and toils...But [the canyon's] walls and cliffs, its peaks and crags...tell a story of beauty and grandeur that I hear yet—and shall continue to hear.

—MAJOR JOHN WESLEY POWELL

HE FIRST DAY OF THE RETURN was hardest. Every foot placement on the steep and slippery trail required concentration, permitting no conversation and little introspection. We were grateful for the distraction of our aching legs and lungs. The act of turning our backs to the river, plunging into the forest and up the mountainside, was a final, symbolic gesture. We had abandoned our hopes for Doug's survival, and although we were convinced that we had done everything possible. our certainty did not assuage an uneasy sense of guilt as the roar of the river faded hourly behind us.

Through occasional breaks in the canopy of the rhododendron forest, we could see behind us, across the river, dense groves of deciduous trees with their color changes now well under way, reds predominant with yellow accents from a birch-like species. Jamie noted: "Surprising how much it does seem like the deepest canyon in the world. When the clouds part, snow and ice and powdered rock appear in the sky, in unexpected places. It is spectacular. I wish I'd never seen it." All of nature's beauty and wonder still soared around us, but something in the core of us was disjointed and we could no longer appreciate what we saw.

A cold rain had settled in by the time we reached the narrow rock ledges that had been our inadequate bivouac shelter on the way down, 500 feet below the knife-edged pass at the top of our route. Now literally within sight of that mysterious line that seemed to define their home territory and security zone, several of the Monpas were almost frantic to press on, and even Tom and Roger felt the pull toward home, no matter how long the journey. Even our former loyalists Squad Leader and Chaplain gestured and yelled in obvious anger when, in late afternoon, I insisted on a halt. To reach the next rock shelter would require roughly six hours of trekking, and we had fixed ropes in two places when we had ascended.

It is an axiom among climbers that most careless accidents occur during descents; they are caused by mental letdown, fatigue, and eagerness to return home after summiting. Horsemen speak of the "horse heading for the barn," and soldiers refer to "short timer's attitude" to explain the erratic and frequently irrational reactions of men in the final days or hours of a difficult tour of combat duty. Now was not the time for haste, a turned ankle, a team member separated. We settled into two damp, disgruntled groups: Americans, Ang Kami, and

Lobsang clustered beneath a small rock overhang on one side of the ravine, and the Monpas gathered beneath another on the far side and a hundred feet above. As darkness swallowed the immense valley beneath our feet, the two campfires winked across the gulf between us like the lights of two ships on a vast and empty ocean.

Dawn arrived with drier weather, better spirits, and Peme Gompa, who, it developed, had raced over the pass in the evening to drop one load and return in the morning for a second. With an irrepressible smile and irresistible resolve, he seized the rucksacks from both Dave and me, lashed them together with a tumpline passed across his forehead, and forged back up the mountainside.

When we crested the pass, we beheld an awe-inspiring and humbling panorama, a sweeping interface of waves of rock and forest, roiling cloud, and glacial ice. It was, Dave recorded, "...a living and moving geological laboratory in which Mother Nature was actively building enormous mountains as she wore their slopes down into soil, a place of both earthquakes and landslides. Tiny, short-lived humans were too frail to be exposed to the forces in operation. We had seen on the outward journey—and heard—and felt—the...explosions of enormous rocks as they literally bounced through a gigantic avalanche chute, leaving the unique smell of crushed rock in their wake as they slammed into one another down a chute where similar crushing falls had occurred thousands, if not millions, of times before we arrived to witness the cataclysmic events. Unfortunately, this dangerous area was on our route of march and we would again have to cross it, with our friends."

As it had on the way out, the saddle on the ridge marked

a dramatic turning point in the Monpas' demeanor. Laughing and joking on the trail picked up as soon as the descent began, and when Ang Kami demonstrated a body rappel down a rope that the others were descending hand-over-hand, he earned a ragged cheer from the youngsters. The changes overtaking the five Americans were less uniform and more gradual, as we each groped to find a balance between our shocking confrontation with Doug's death and our return to the living, breathing, everyday world.

"I kept being surprised that ordinary life went on, somehow mocking the significance of what had happened," Jamie recalled. "How petty…stale and tired seemed the details of camp life, of keeping up, of not straying too far ahead either…of route-finding and slipping and nettles and leeches…the constant fatigue that I carried around like an extra pack. But the most surprising ordinary life of all was in my own head: the worry that I wasn't measuring up, that the Monpas weren't impressed with my stamina, that I wasn't being sensitive enough to them, or to Tom, that I was being too delicate, too moody, too abstracted, that we should have kept going, that I wasn't taking good pictures.

"How could I think of such things, in the shadow of that huge event, that shutting off of the great binary gate that separates the living from the dead? I even laughed, at times. I made jokes. I smiled at others' jokes. Every time, it seemed strange, disrespectful, wrong. But to not do so seemed artificial, and so even more wrong. Worst of all, the greatest disrespect, would be to fake it, to put on some unreal attitude or emotion. The event was there, in my mind, like some huge thundercloud, while all of the niggling insecurities and tiresome details of daily life played out beneath or beside or within it....˝

FOR EACH OF US THE SHIFT BACK TO ORDINARY CONCERNS CAME at a different pace. I struggled to separate feelings of genuine and justified anger at Village Voice's attempts to take advantage of our emergency, from my petty resentment of the young Monpas, who joked, laughed, hunted, and in general behaved as teenagers would anywhere if they did not know the victim and had little experience with mortality.

Fortunately for the group dynamics, Tom and Roger were better able to react on dual levels, and their warm relationship with the young men was less affected by their own grief and physical debilitation. For all his sometimes dour and remote demeanor, Tom has an understanding and extroverted way with teenagers, often seeming to find more value and reality in their bright passion and clear vision than in more turbid adult life. Our first night after crossing the pass, bivouacked again beneath the two boulders where they had shot the first takin on the way out, with bellies once again full of the sausage they had cached, the Monpas stayed up late with Tom around a blazing fire, eagerly singing songs and exchanging vocabulary words and phrases.

Suddenly, at two minutes after ten in the evening, with a roar like a landing jet, came an abrupt reminder of the vast orogenic forces at work around us, and again our great predecessor Kingdon Ward had been there before and described it with accuracy and eloquence we could not match:

> ...a most extraordinary rumbling noise broke out, and the earth began to shudder violently. Shattering the dead silence of the night in that remote mountain retreat, the

ominous rumble swelled to a deafening roar. It was as though the keystone had fallen out of the universe and the arch of the sky were collapsing.

The night was black, for there was no moon, but I remember seeing a dark ridge silhouetted against a planet-powdered ribbon of sky become fuzzy for a moment. The whole bristling edge of forest was shaking violently.... These solid mountains were in the grip of a force that was shaking them as a terrier shakes a rat....

The earthquake roared on. Something was pounding the ground beneath us with the force of a giant sledge hammer. Our once-solid ground felt like no more than a thin covering stretched across the valley floor and attached by its edges to the mountains. It seemed that the very foundations of the world were breaking up under the violent blows, that the crust on which we lay would crumple like an ice floe in a rough sea and hurl us into a bottomless pit.

Besides the roaring of the earthquake itself there was another more familiar sound—the crash of rock avalanches pouring into the gorge as cliffs broke in half and boulders poured down a hundred scuppers with a clatter and a rumble.

...But presently the battering ceased, and the noise died away except for an occasional avalanche. Then without warning came four or five sharp explosions in quick succession, seemingly high up in the dark sky. They sounded like ack-ack *shells bursting. It was the ceasefire; everything became quiet, and the madness was over for a while.* [2]

The 1950 earthquake that Kingdon Ward described from a campsite about 150 miles southeast of our "takin camp" bivouac was vastly greater than the tremor that shook us on October 24, 1998; at 8.6 on the Richter scale, Kingdon Ward's quake was one of the most violent ever recorded. In conversations the next morning, however, we concluded that no earthquake is minor when you are lying in the dark under the overhung sides of a boulder perched like a 50-ton bowling ball on a slope dropping precipitously several thousand feet into the inner gorge of the Tsangpo.

By the following day, as our group crossed the next ridge and dropped toward the misty, magical valley of Nadang, we had assumed a natural order of march. In front went Peme Gompa and Point Mar, finding the way. Close on their heels came the other porters, surging forward quickly for an hour or so, then downing their loads for long cigarette breaks: at midmorning and mid-afternoon, hastily built fires produced tea as well. Near the front walked Tom and Roger, while Ang Kami Sherpa ranged nearby, sometimes following the Monpas's route and sometimes taking a parallel course.

Alone with his thoughts and his efforts to regain his strength, Jamie walked "in the middle, between fast Tom and Roger and slow Wick and Dave, where I could be alone, without fear of falling behind, or competition to keep up. Although I had spent only a little more than one day lying in my bag under a tarp, rolling away to retch into the sand, I felt in the next days, hiking out, as if I were recovering from a long illness or major surgery."

Dave and I brought up the rear, accompanied by Lobsang, who scouted just ahead to keep track of the trail and halted at each steep pitch to extend an iron-hard helping arm. The slowest walkers in any case, Dave and I were not immune to the physical drain affecting us all. We both experienced occasional dizzy spells when we looked upward at the horizon, and these were the result, Dave conjectured, of dehydration. Bruised ribs from a fall exacerbated Dave's painful breathing, already labored from a combination of mild asthma and altitude, and he estimated he was now 20 pounds lighter than he was when we had trekked down the Po Tsangpo short weeks before.

Dave and I meekly accepted our slow and sometimes painful progress. The Monpas had been born here, were 30 and more years our juniors, had hundreds fewer parachute jumps recorded in their knees. Tom's mind does not work that way. Surreptitiously making sure his rucksack was at least as heavy as the Monpas's loaded bamboo baskets, he placed himself at the front and resolved to learn how these scrawny fellows could cover the terrain so efficiently. Noticing his intent scrutiny and obvious interest, Peme Gompa adopted him "like a little brother," Tom later recalled, and taught him as he might a youngster on a first hunt.

Peme Gompa demonstrated how he turned his toes outward on steep, muddy uphill pitches, like a cross-country skier doing a herringbone, and showed Tom how to throw his weight forward with hips slightly turned when going down. Requesting Ang Kami to translate, Peme Gompa emphasized that "you must take responsibility for every step in the mountains. You cannot allow yourself to be sloppy; it is not automatic."

Tom found it perfectly natural to be relearning how to walk at age 52, not because of some catastrophic accident but because he had never learned it well enough before. He threw himself into the opportunity with all the intensity we had applied as teenagers to learning perfect paddle strokes on slalom courses. He would enjoy sharing his new skill with descendants of the Maya in the next remote Mexican canyon he visited.

Even this newly discovered passion for walking technique could not distract Tom for long from the difficult, sometimes unanswerable questions that were nagging at us, challenging us to understand our individual roles in and responsibilities for the tragedy that had taken Doug's life. Images of the accident would return unbidden, along with mental replays of other incidents and conversations, of discussions about risk, procedures, and equipment—not just from this trip but from other years and other rivers.

Tom would never know what had thwarted Doug's calculations that fatal morning. Had Doug been injured as his boat thrashed in the first hole, weakening his Eskimo roll attempts? Had he become dislodged from the bracing holding him securely in the boat? Had the weight of gear in the boat shifted or otherwise compromised his balance? Or had some unmentioned illness or injury reduced his concentration or ability without his realizing it? These and other possibilities would recur and recur with flashbacks to those first, long, terrible seconds of the accident, always without answer.

We had some comfort in knowing that Doug, to the end, was exercising the personal judgment and freedom he valued so highly. He ran the ledge by the route of his own choosing, simply because he wanted to run it and was certain he could; he was not reacting to any peer pressure or problem they had gotten into as a team. The carry-around was faster than the time it took to scout and prepare to run the drop, and Tom and Roger had already elected to walk. Everyone felt they were finally making good progress, so they had taken all the time they felt they needed to scout from all angles.

Beyond that simple core of facts, however, loomed a constellation of questions with answers difficult to arrive at or to accept. Tom asked himself if he could have been a better leader on the river. Had he guided the group consensus to an appropriate balance of boldness and conservatism? Had he succeeded in his quiet talks with the others, including Doug, about maintaining a calm and steady approach? Had they made the right decision to enter the gorge with boats? Did their last-minute decision to carry the weight of five-days extra food affect the outcome?

Roger walked within sight of Tom and the leading Monpas, but he seldom spoke, as lost as Tom in his own introspection. About the accident, Roger's questions were specific. Should he have spoken out against the run Doug attempted, as they scouted together just moments before? Should he have expressed even more clearly to the others his sense of the danger they all faced? Could he somehow have helped Doug make the bracing in his boat more secure?

More of his silent dialogue, however, concerned the great, unknowable "what ifs." They had looked at this route for an escape if they could not make Rainbow Falls as planned, and on the map back at Gyala it had seemed straightforward. Now Roger looked around at the immense, convoluted terrain and wondered how they could have managed if Dave and I had not been at Panther Beach with the Monpas. If Doug had successfully made the move at the last ledge, as he and everyone else confidently expected, would they have continued on until someone else came to grief?

Jamie's mind wandered farther, from an imaginary conversation with Paulo about the accident to detailed planning
of a long "follow the fall" canoe-camping trip with his family
south from the Arctic Circle. He noted in his journal, however,
that the reveries never lasted long before the Tsangpo snatched
him back:

> *I found that I couldn't talk and walk at the same time.
> Yes, like an old joke. And if I worried that I wasn't keep-
> ing up—or felt proud that I was ahead—either way,
> either humility or pride leadeth to a fall. If I daydreamed,
> or dwelt on home and family, I would stumble. If I for-
> got to look ahead, stared only at my feet, I would walk
> to the edge of a steep drop, or into an unclimbable wall.*
>
> *Naturally I felt sorry and sad for Doug, and for
> Connie, and Tyler and Bryce. And a little bit sorry for
> me, too, and for Sandra, and Bruce, and all of Doug's
> friends. But the other thing I felt was disorientation.
> Imagine, say, that you have built up a firm political opin-
> ion, over your lifetime, and then you visit some country
> or read a new book and realize that everything you've
> believed was wrong.*
>
> *I had believed in Doug's judgment, his superb ration-
> ality, his caution, his good sense.... I had staked my life on
> that belief, more than once. Once that was swept away—
> literally and figuratively—I doubted everything. I doubted
> the people around me. Most of all I doubted my own judg-
> ment. But what else can you rely on, out there in the wilder-
> ness...but on your own judgment? You can't think about
> every footstep; you have to believe in order to move.*

Bringing up the rear, I asked myself if I could have been a better leader and whether I should have planned and led the expedition at all. I had spent years putting together a high-risk enterprise that had resulted in a tragic and wasteful death. Did my pretrip rationale that I was creating opportunities for my friends—even paying back the sport, now that I was retired from active paddling, by contributing my experience, organizational skills, and leadership ability—have a tinny ring of fatuous conceit?

Did my low-key approach to the Chinese in obtaining permits possibly cut us off from earlier and better information about the floods and also lock us into a less flexible schedule than we might otherwise have negotiated? Should I not have chosen to cut myself out of the decision process on going beyond Gyala with boats?

In the face of the awful finality of Doug's death and the immensity of the natural forces surrounding it, obsessing on one's personal role seemed egotistical and unworthy, yet failing to understand and embrace that individual responsibility seemed an even greater betrayal of one of the clearest and most honest thinkers any of us had ever known. The questions revolved endlessly, while the answers shifted, forming and transforming themselves like the banks of clouds through which we walked down into the bowl of Nadang.

Dave and I forded the glacial stream at Nadang, where we had been taught to perform the ritual face washing on the way in, and emerged with ice water streaming from our pant legs, chilled feet painfully walking on the irregular rock debris. For a hundred yards along a dry gravel bar, relic of the melting snowfields of spring and summer, lay strewn packs and bamboo baskets—every bit of our equipment and supplies. My instant thought was of the more lurid illustrations accompanying Stanley's accounts of his Congo expeditions, dozens of porters dropping their loads and running off into the bush to strand the explorer in deepest Africa.

Tom and Roger quickly arrived to disabuse me, describing how they had crossed the stream 40 minutes previously with the Monpas. Suddenly, without a word or any cue the two Americans could see or hear, every one of the Monpas had frozen in mid-stride. On a curt command from Feme Gompa, all dropped their packs where they stood and raced downstream, loading rifles as they ran. After ten minutes of silence, several shots echoed at a distance. Shortly the three youngest hunters returned to retrieve butchering tools from the discarded packs, jubilantly telling Ang Kami they had surrounded and killed five takins.

The Monpas rejoined us in the morning, all traces of anxiety now gone. Their only remaining concerns were the logistics of getting us, our equipment, and this new bounty of meat and hides to Mendung village as rapidly as possible. We were equally eager to go on, and a persistent cold rain did not encourage lingering in any case. A pale glacier loomed out of the fog like the prow of an ocean liner beside the pass leading from the Nadang bowl; another minor earthquake shook the hills in the night; and the stream under the three-log bridge at Kingdon Ward's crossing now pulsed angrily with rainwater. In two days we hastened down the trail that had taken us four on the outbound journey, and late in the afternoon of October 27 we climbed gratefully up the notched log ladder into the dry luxury of Peme Gompa's house.

Before I could even shed my pack, a messenger handed me one of the brightly colored waterproof sacks in which we protected all our important gear. It came from Paulo, and within were two precious, fully charged satellite-telephone batteries. The sack also held a note explaining that the previously closed road in the avalanche zone was now open to limited traffic, but Paulo had been unable to trek down the Po Tsangpo trail to meet us. The recent seismic tremors had broken loose a huge section of rain-saturated hillside, and the trail was cut between us and the road.

Villagers confirmed that the trail was cut and added that it would be subject to further slides if the rain continued to saturate the unvegetated slope. Climbing safely above the unstable zone would, they said, add another two days to the trek out. Wait for a break in the weather, they advised. Besides, the following day there was to be a housewarming in Mendung to celebrate construction of a new dwelling, and no one seemed eager to miss a good party to porter loads up to the road if the work could be postponed. We determined to take this last delay with as much grace as possible, although by now everyone was thinking increasingly of home. Veteran traveler Dave recorded in his journal: "I find my daydreams alternating between Susan and ham and eggs—all of which have taken on immense importance to me over the past month."

Several of our Lost Boys were already hanging around Peme Gompa's porch with more than casual interest when I arrived, and before we worried about anything else the crew needed to be paid. They had received nothing to date and were understandably eager for their big payday. Dave and I shut ourselves in Peme Gompa's little altar room to escape curious eyes, checked our count of days and rates three times, and dealt out the money. Determined not to let Village Voice's attempts to take advantage of us pass unremarked, I also summoned up all my righteous indignation and composed a short but devastating denunciation of his behavior.

I should have saved my eloquence, and Ang Kami's breath. All eyes were fixed on the three-inch-thick pile of hundred-yuan banknotes, and my words did as little good as most morality lectures. Even my American comrades were unimpressed.

On October 27, 1998, Jamie McEwan wrote in his journal: "*...scene with paying the Monpas was a flop. Wick's speech was short, anticlimactic. I took a roll of film—mostly of counting money.*" Dave Phillips, in his journal, wrote: "*A great effort, but it probably did as much good as a lecture to a wayward teenager.*"

In my own journal, I recorded these words: "*Unfortunately not the dramatic response I expected—although I also didn't eat a machete, so not all bad.*"

The fact was that all of us had turned our focus to the future; those hard memories less than two weeks old were already from a remote place and time.

The following day, Tom took the next step to break our public silence, calling National Public Radio from Mendung and taping a second interview for broadcast two days later. Like the first, from the put-in at Pei, this interview was short and simplistic. It reinforced the clear statement we had already released, but it added nothing more and had the unfortunate result of advertising the fact that we had suffered a death on the river far beyond the white-water paddling community.

Meanwhile, in Potomac, Maryland, Sarah Park was under increasing pressure for more information. Reporters from newspapers and magazines tried to elicit comments for quotation, our satellite-telephone numbers, interviews with family members, even details on our flight arrangements home. Harder to ignore were the uninformed rumors and accusations rippling around the Internet. Some questioning our judgment were simply annoying, but others need to be quickly squelched. One of them said that we were all trapped and in imminent peril in the gorge, and that rumor might have created needless concern both for our families and friends and also for the Chinese government.

Not to be ignored, however, were two expeditions generously offering help and asking for advice. They needed to know what they could do and, more important, what additional risks need not be taken. One was the expedition by Ian Baker, Ken Storm, and Hamid Sardar, scheduled to trek into the gorge within days to explore on foot the right bank not far downstream from where we had searched unsuccessfully for Doug and his equipment. The other group was a Spanish mountaineering team at that moment on Gyala Pelri. They planned to scout down the right bank of the Tsangpo below Gyala after their climb, preparing for a possible kayak expedition in the future. Both needed to know what areas we had searched. We also wanted them to understand that—while any evidence of Doug's death they came across should of course be recorded and reported—we considered taking additional risks unjustified.

Tom began drafting a more detailed report for distribution to our friends by e-mail, but we dared not release it prior to the official Chinese accident investigation (which concluded on November 5 with a finding of death, not "missing" status). Meanwhile, for a few more days we would remain insulated from the wider world behind the twin barricades of Sarah and Harry.

By mid-morning the village was astir with preparations for the housewarming. Work crews swarmed over the new dwelling, fastening the final, lapped rows of wooden roof shingles, cleaning up construction debris from the barnyard, sweeping the floor of the single large family room. Several hundred yards away, four women at an open-air kitchen boiled and stir-fried unidentifiable delicacies in huge pots, which were then transferred to a wheeled handcart for delivery across the village. Children gathered in wide-eyed, whispering groups to watch the proceedings. From just beyond stone-throwing range, dogs kept track of food deliveries, workers, and the children.

The party was in full swing by the time we arrived at the new house about 5:30 p.m., with 30 or more people of all ages packed into the smoke-filled great room. Women wore bright blouses and dark skirts, some topping the ensemble with green Chinese fatigue caps. The younger men favored military surplus camouflage, accented with silver-sheathed belt knives. Smoke curled upward from the new hearth in one corner, and the massive central post supporting the roof was wrapped with dozens of white scarves, a Tibetan symbol for hospitality.

A bewildering number of wives and children were presented to us by the men who had accompanied us on the trail; even Village Voice solemnly showed off his infant son. Homemade rice wine was generously dispensed from a rectangular plastic jerry can, and several of the revelers began singing, women and men alternating verses of folk songs. Some we could recognize from Tom and Roger's sessions with the Lost Boys beneath the rock shelters. There were no musical instruments, but the clear voices easily carried the rhythmic melody.

Young women congregated in one corner, young men in another. Eventually one of the women, perhaps less inhibited or more inebriated than her peers, initiated a rollicking dance. As they sang their verse of a song, three or four of the women, with arms linked, surged forward and around the scarf-draped central post, and then they retired as the men surged forward in their turn. The jerry can of home brew circulated, and the tempo of the songs and dances increased along with the heat and smoke of the crowded room.

With middle-aged decorum, we slipped out of the party early and retired to Peme Gompa's. For once, his hearth was not the gathering spot of the neighborhood, and we spent a quiet evening with him and his immediate family. To Peme Gompa we presented several useful items of expedition equipment and a cash payment for our freehanded use of his house (in lieu of a bonus for the trip, which we feared might create further resentment among the others). To his wife we bequeathed the expedition's entire supply of jams and honey, brought from Kathmandu and intended for use while camping, but loaded by mistake with the supplies carried down the Po Tsangpo.

Also in the supplies that had come this far but no farther were the last few inches from a bottle of Johnnie Walker scotch I had bought duty free in London. I passed a healthy dollop to Peme Gompa, who took a thoughtful sniff and taste, then flashed a delighted grin and eagerly poured exactly half the measure for his wife. Peme Gompa returned the favor by offering home brew from his jerry can, of course, and Dave, ever the gentleman, stayed with him cup for cup. From the corner where I was taking photographs, I could see Dave surreptitiously pouring each teacup of oily, clear liquid through a crack in the floorboards, and I wondered if the family's 300-pound sow was standing in the cattle shed beneath, mouth agape, enjoying the party, too.

The following day we found that the partying villagers had not been exaggerating. The landslide cutting the path up the Po Tsangpo was serious, and in wet weather it would indeed have been too unstable to attempt. Where the solid footpath had traversed along the right side, 600 feet above the rapids of the Po Tsangpo, there now lay a steep scalloped gouge of unstable broken rock and mud 300 feet across, extending farther than we could see above and directly into the river below. Except where islands of tangled, uprooted trees protruded from the jumble, it dropped smoothly and uninterrupted, pitched as steeply as a roof. Occasionally a small stone broke loose and clattered a few feet before coming to rest again, but the day was sunny and the drying slope seemed settled for the moment.

More intimidating than difficult, the route across the slide was a series of scratched-out footholds, most smaller than a boot sole. We angled our walking sticks across our chests to dig into the slope at our left and stepped carefully across. A constant mental effort was required to keep our bodies away from the slope and our weight pressed vertically downward, for the natural instinct to hug the wall would have shot our boots right off their narrow placements. Nowhere was Peme Gompa's advice about taking responsibility for every footstep more true, and with care we crossed without incident.

We made camp shortly after we crossed the landslide, and a three-hour march the following morning brought us at noon to the last of the trembling, undulating, loosely planked suspension bridges high above the river, rows of tall white prayer flags rippling on either side. On the far side stood two white Land Cruisers, drivers eager to transport us back to Lhasa. Sunlight flashed off the lens of Paulo's video camera as we stepped out of the time machine.

EPILOGUE

ON A BRISK, PALE-SUNNED SATURDAY in late November, more than two hundred of Doug Gordon's family and friends gathered from all over the United States at a simple, white Grange Hall outside Cornwall, Connecticut. In the style of a Quaker meeting, chosen to reflect the informality, individuality, and spontaneity Doug valued, participants rose as the spirit moved them to share their grief and celebrate his memory. Over the course of two hours, more than 30 of those closest to him spoke in succession, some from notes, some extemporaneously, some with tears and some with humor. Anecdotes ranged from river tales, whitewater runs and racing, to family life, scientific research, pranks and parties, covering the span from his birth to his loss on the Tsangpo.

The common threads, through all the poignant stories in Cornwall and other eulogies written in the months thereafter, were not the many and varied achievements of his remarkable talent, but the way he lived and influenced so many others to experience life in so many dimensions:

> "... after the accident, our experience changed dramatically. We were there for the adventure of seeing this enormous river canyon, these huge mountains. Before the

*accident, we marveled everyday at the snowcapped moun-
tains that would appear suddenly through the clouds,
25,000 feet high, beautiful vistas, glaciers that came down
to the water. Around every turn it was magnificent … .
And afterwards, the scenery didn't change – it was just
as magnificent—but it was empty. …We never saw
[Doug] again after the accident and a beautiful trip that
he would have enjoyed and relished, he was not there to
share it with us. … I'm sure that many here will have
the same experience of missing, in your lives, his companionship and his participation."*

—Tom McEwan

"[Albert Einstein] *thought that God was in all things
that were held sacred and even inspirational by man –
from the simplest everyday task to the truly holy. … Perhaps the beauty of that one fast and clean run, better than
anyone could imagine, was and is one of the racer's con-
nections to God. Perhaps Doug's God drew him to those
places where his experience on the river felt almost holy."*

—Ken Stone,

United States Slalom Team Coach

"*I …never met a boater who was as solid as Doug; he
was just where he wanted to be, all the time. …He had
as long a racing career as I can remember anyone having, at an extremely high level. But after he stopped racing, he kept kayaking. That was ten years ago. Ten years,
and Doug never stopped exploring. His purpose was to
go to the wildest places. He wasn't doing it to be famous*

or to be the one that everyone would look up to – many paddlers haven't heard of him – but I think he was seeking out the most true form of exploration that there is."

—Landis Arnold, boating friend

"He believed that if you saw the line and knew you could make it, you shouldn't let fear get the better of you. On the other hand, he also realized that if he was having a bad day, he needed to be more conservative than usual. He was someone whose judgement I respected immensely."

—Bruce Lessels, boating friend

"Doug's ability to marvel at life's unexpected moments and to embrace whatever challenges presented themselves was infectious and invigorating. He never stopped thinking, challenging himself and those around him, encouraging all of us to reach a little further, and enjoy life a little more than we would otherwise have done. I learned a lot from Doug, about levers, about sportsmanship, about the bond between fun and work, and most of all about the bond between friends ...."

—David Halpern, classmate

"And now he's gone, and I need an explanation for that. Doug would have been quick to provide one. I am slower. But after much thought I realized that he is, like all of you listening to this, a personification of the adventuresome spirit that is necessary to accomplish things in this world."

—Bill Endicott,
United States Whitewater Team Coach

*"He didn't just think his way down the river or what-
ever [else] he was doing, but he experienced it more fully
than most people ever do. And that's why it's so hard for
me, and I think for everyone, to realize that he's not here
—he's gone—because he seemed more alive, more awake
..., both thinking more about what was around him, feeling more all at the same time. ... As I remember him, I'll
...hold him not just as a memory, but as a kind of ideal."*
                                            —JAMIE McEWAN

"We ... were prepared for almost anything," wrote Frank Kingdon
Ward in 1926 of his exploration of the Tsangpo Gorges with
Lord Cawdor, *"except the possibility of failure ...."*[1]

In the immediate aftermath of Doug's death and the cur-
tailment of the expedition, Jamie spoke for us all when he
wrote from Lhasa that given the outcome, he now wished we
had never come to Tibet, never attempted the Tsangpo. Our
goals and ambitions were not remotely worth the life that had
been lost.

While the death of a team member was our paramount failure, it was not the only one. We also fell far short of our dream
and acknowledged goal, to accomplish a first white-water
descent of the Tsangpo gorges. The paddlers traversed but 35
miles of river, 18 of which were the warm-up from Pei to Gyala.
We had calculated before the trip that the first 72 miles were
the minimum that we would consider the major white-water
challenge. Before the team left Gyala that ambition had been
radically curtailed, and even had the tragedy not occurred the
most that we might have accomplished in 1998 would have
been another ten miles of river descent, followed by abandon-

ing the boats and exiting on foot, along the left side of the unexplored inner canyon.

Yet, just as defining success on a first river descent is a subjective and elusive task, so, we found, is defining failure. Tom and I never lost our fundamental conviction that Doug, like us, had lived to be in wild places, to see and experience places like the Tsangpo. Before our departure in September, in the welter of analyzing satellite imagery, packaging food, finalizing air tickets, choosing climbing equipment, changing money, and a thousand other details, Doug wrote down three goals with elegant simplicity: "survive, experience, enjoy,"

Doug had been quick to point out that "to survive' was a collective, team goal, not just a personal objective. The loss of any team member was equally unacceptable, and it was unacceptable not because of its effect on the one lost, but precisely because of its effect on the galaxy of survivors: family most of all, but also friends, professional colleagues and, of course, fellow expedition members.

"To experience" had a deeper, richer meaning than simply to traverse the gorge, to run the white water, to be the first. It meant crossing that divide into coexistence with the environment: walking and living in rock shelters with the Monpas; holding and balancing on the steep rock, breathing the moist, pungent cloud forest air. Most of all, to the paddlers it meant flowing with the mighty river. Yet always there were limits, frequently difficult to discern, beyond which we should not venture.

"To enjoy" likewise had broader scope than its often flabby connotation. It meant to keep all the senses open, to realize the experience in all its wonder, to savor all the human emotions:

joys of companionship and teamwork, awe of the immense landscape, triumph in successes, but also fear of the challenges. Here too danger and risk were part of the warp of the richly textured fabric.

Now with the hindsight of months, not days, all of us, his companions from the expedition, are beginning to perceive our time in the Tsangpo gorges by all three of Doug's criteria, not solely the first. We along with Doug experienced deeply one of the planet's greatest, wildest regions, and we enjoyed keenly the teamwork, skills, and physical demands it required of us. Those are things to be savored and valued, not negated by the devastation of his death.

And whether it is our lot to return to court the Diamond Sow again, or whether that privilege falls to others, perhaps we will be wise enough to emulate Eric Shipton, who, ten years before Edmund Hillary and Tenzing Norgay triumphed on Everest, reflected on his own repeatedly frustrated attempts:

> *No, it is not remarkable that Everest did not yield to the first few attempts; indeed, it would have been very surprising and not a little sad if it had, for that is not the way of great mountains. Perhaps we had become a little arrogant with our fine new technique of ice-claw and rubber slipper, our age of easy mechanical conquest. We had forgotten that the mountain still holds the master card, that it will grant success only in its own good time. Why else does mountaineering retain its deep fascination?*
>
> *It is possible, even probable, that in time men will look back with wonder at our feeble efforts, unable to account for our repeated failure, while they themselves are grappling with far more formidable problems. If we*

are still alive we shall no doubt mumble fiercely in our grey beards in a desperate effort to justify our weakness. But if we are wise we shall reflect with deep gratitude that we seized our mountaineering heritage, and will take pleasure in watching younger men enjoy theirs. [2]

Notes and Sources

Author's Note: This narrative is a synthesis of my personal experiences, those of my companions in Tibet and elsewhere, and a wide body of literature concerning everything from the history of exploration in Asia to satellite communications and imagery. In the interest of producing an uncluttered, readable text I have limited footnotes primarily to direct quotes and extracts. For readers interested in more detail on particular topics, especially those planning similar efforts, I have also listed below the sources I found most useful.

DEDICATION
- [1]Walker, Wick. "South by Simple." *Coleman Outdoor Adventures,* 1987.
- For more on Tamul Falls, see Walker, Wick. "Treasure of the Sierra Madre." *Canoe.* May 1987.
- McEwan, Jamie. "Santa Maria!" *First Descents, In Search of Wild Rivers.* Birmingham: Menasha Ridge Press, 1989.

PREFACE
- [1]Ward, Captain F. Kingdon. *The Riddle of the Tsangpo Gorges.* London: Edward Arnold, 1926. pp. 224-225
- Bailey, F.M. "Note on the Falls of the Tsang-Po." *The Scottish Geographical Magazine,* vol.XXX., February 1914.
- McRae, Michael. "Racing for Shangri-La, Tibet's Tsangpo Gorge." *Earth's Mystical Grand Canyons.* Tucson:

Sunracer Publications, 1995.

Chapter I

◆ [1]Davis, Mark. *Lost in the Grand Canyon*. The American Experience, Public Broadcasting Service, 1999.

Chapter II

For an account of the first descents of the Yangtze, see:

◆ [1]Bangs, Richard, and Kallen, Christian. *Riding the Dragon's Back, The Race to Raft the Upper Yangtze*. New York: Laurel, 1982.

For details of the 1981 Bhutan expedition, see:

◆ Evans, Eric. "Paddling the Land of the Thunder Dragon." *Canoe*, May/June, 1982.

◆ Haupt, Donna E. "Rapture of the Rapids." *Life*, November, 1982.

◆ Wick Walker. "Final Report of the American Himalayan Kayak Descent." Unpublished, 1982 distribution: American Canoe Association; Canoe Cruisers Association, Washington, D.C.; Alpiner Kanu Club, Munich; Bhutan Travel Agency, N.Y.; Himal Venture, Darjeeling.

Chapter III

◆ [1]Powell, J.W. p. 247.

◆ [2]Shipton, Eric. "Nanda Devi." *Eric Shipton The Six Mountain Travel Books*. Seattle: The Mountaineers, 1985.

Chapter IV

◆ [1]From Kinthup's letter to his British superiors at the Great Trigonometrical Survey in Darjeeling. Waller sources this to

Records of the Survey of India, vol.8, part 2: "Kinthup's Narrative of a Journey from Darjeeling to Gyala Sindong (Gyala and Sengdam), Tsari and the Lower Tsang-po, 1880-84. Compiled by Col. H.C.B. Tanner."

◆ [2]Waddell, L.A. *Among the Himalayas.* London, 1900. p.66

◆ [3]Waller, Derek. *The Pundits, British Exploration of Tibet & Central Asia.* Lexington: The University Press of Kentucky, 1990. p. 228.

◆[4]Bowl and fields and shimmering mountains remain, of course. The dzong (fort) has been pulled down in the intervening years, and today its stone walls have been rebuilt into a prosperous single story farm complex.

◆[5]Kinthup's account, and consequently the published descriptions of his route, are vague, but from setting them beside the actual lay of the land it seems clear that he fled down the tributary Rong Chu to the Po Tsangpo, and thence to the Tsangpo in the vicinity of the confluence at Gompo Ne. Bailey (see below), the only reporter other than the Indian transcriber of his report actually to talk to Kinthup, reported in separate descriptions that Kinthup rejoined the Tsangpo at "the village of Dorjiyu Dzong" and at a point "just downstream from Pemakochung." Bailey was unfortunately never able to explore down the Po Tsangpo, for summer floods had destroyed the bridges the year he was there. From the author's two trips into the area, as well as modern satellite photography, it appears clear that the first location even feasible for a village after Pemakochung lies in the vicinity of the sacred site of Gompo Ne just downstream from the confluence of the Po Tsangpo and the Tsangpo. Here the modern villages of

Zhachu and Mendung occupy hillsides a thousand feet above the rivers, and an odd pattern of thick, almost impenetrable and likely second growth vegetation adjoins the painted cliffs and religious symbols at the uninhabited riverside religious site. While satellites now reveal that dramatic, tectonic zig-zags force the river to flow about 23 miles, some yet to be seen by Western eyes, between Pemakochung and Gompo Ne, the direct distance is but nine miles, thus aptly fitting Bailey's description.

◆ [6]From near the Marpung Monastary, at the modern village of Medog, the Doshung La (pass) cuts across the base of the Tsangpo's great horseshoe bend, a relatively easy three day walk that bypasses 140 miles of the almost impenetrable gorges, as well as giving Tongkyuk Dzong a wide birth.

◆ [7]Kinthup did accompany one more Pundit mission, but with unremarkable results.

◆ [8]Bailey, F.M. *No Passport to Tibet*. London: Rupert Hart-Davis, 1957. p. 143.

◆ [9]Although frequently flouted, Chinese regulations in 1998 forbade import and use of unlicensed satellite telephones. With our hard won and tenuous permits at stake, as well as time and thousands of dollars invested, we feared committing any violations that might give authorities reason to cancel our plans. This proved a fortunate choice, since in the aftermath of the tragedy our use of the phones to make official reports and notify kin was obvious, and the source of the phones was one question asked by authorities.

◆ [10]Under pressure from commercial European satellite imaging companies. the United States in the mid-1990's began liberalizing classifications and restrictions on civilian use of satellite technology. The implications for science, engineering, agriculture, and other applications are staggering, and only beginning to emerge. Nowhere will the effects be greater than in wilderness exploration. The first American company founded specifically to serve civilian needs, Space Imaging, Inc. of Thornton, Colorado, sponsored our expedition by providing custom produced photomaps and profiles of the Tsangpo's gradient.

For a broad overview of "The Great Game," see:

◆ Hopkirk, Peter. *The Great Game, The Struggle for Empire in Central Asia*. New York: Kodansha America, Inc., 1992.

◆ Meyer, Karl E. and Brysac, Shareen Blair. *Tournament of Shadows, The Great Game and the Race for Empire in Central Asia*. Washington, D.C.: Counterpoint, 1999.

For the history of western exploration in Tibet see:

◆ Allen, Charles. *A Mountain in Tibet, The Search for Mount Kailas and the Sources of the Great Rivers of India*. London: Futura Publications, 1983.

◆ Hopkirk, Peter. *Trespassers on the Roof of the World, The Race for Lhasa*. Oxford: Oxford University Press, 1983.

For an account of Hayward's murder in Yasin, see:

◆ Keay, John. *The Gilgit Game, The Explorers of the Western Himalayas 1865-95*. Hamden, Connecticut: Archon Books, 1979.

For the history of "The Pundits," including detailed accounts of Kinthup and Bailey, see:

◆ Waller, Derek. *The Pundits, British Exploration of Tibet & Central Asia*. Lexington: The University Press of Kentucky, 1990.

For Bailey's expedition in particular, see:

◆ Bailey, F.M. *No Passport to Tibet.* London: Rupert Hart-Davis, 1957.

◆ "Note on the Falls of the Tsang-Po." *The Scottish Geographical Magazine,* vol.xxx., February 1914.

CHAPTER V

◆ [1]Young, Geoffrey Winthrop. "Introduction to Upon That Mountain." *Eric Shipton The Six Mountain Travel Books.* Seattle: The Mountaineers, 1985. p. 313

◆ [3]Clarke, Mark. Memorial Service, Cornwall, CT, November 21, 1998.

◆ [4]Powell, J.W. p. 218.

◆ [5]French, Patrick. *Younghusband, The Last Great Imperial Adventurer.* London: Harper Collins, 1994.

◆ [6]Gordon, Douglas. "The Dean River, Kayaking in the Land of the Grizzly." *Kanawa,* August/September/October, 1997.

◆ [2]It was, for instance, a nuclear physicist and World Champion in canoe slalom, Natan Bernot, who introduced the European idea of specialized, totally enclosed, white-water canoes to the United States, at Pennsylvania State University in 1961.

CHAPTER VI

◆ [1]The Khampa are a notoriously independent and warlike group originating in eastern Tibet, who formed the backbone of the guerilla resistance to Chinese occupation in the 1950's. For details see:

◆ Knaus, John Kenneth. *Orphans of the Cold War.* New York: Public Affairs, 1999.

◆ Logan, Pamela. *Among Warriors.* New York: Vintage

Departures, 1998.

◆ [2]Bailey, F.M. *No Passport to Tibet.* London: Rupert Hart-Davis, 1957. pp.269-271.

◆ [3]Ward, Captain F. Kingdon. *The Riddle of the Tsangpo Gorges.* London: Edward Arnold, 1926. pp. 234-235.

◆ [4]Ibid. pp. xiii-xiv.

◆ [5]Ibid. pp. 238-241.

CHAPTER VII

◆ [1]Powell, J.W. p. 212.

CHAPTER VIII

◆ [1]Barrie, James Matthew, Sir, Bart. *Peter Pan.* New York: Charles Scribner's Sons, 1980. p. 40.

◆ [2]Ward, Captain F. Kingdon. *The Riddle of the Tsangpo Gorges.* London: Edward Arnold, 1926. pp. 242-242.

◆ [3]ibid. p. 244.

CHAPTER IX

◆ [1]Noyce, Wilfrid. *The Quotable Climber.* New York: The Lyons Press, 1998. p. 77.

◆ [2]McEwan, Jamie. "Whitewater to Die for." *AMC Outdoors,* March 1998.

◆ [3]Gordon, Douglas. "They Don't Come Any Better." *American Whitewater,* September/October, 1997.

◆ [4]Bailey, F.M. *No Passport to Tibet.* London: Rupert Hart-Davis, 1957. p. 9.

CHAPTER X

◆ [1]Unsoeld, Willi. *The Quotable Climber.* New York: The Lyons

Press, 1998. p. 77.

◆ [2] Words: Eleanor Farjeon; Music: Traditional Gaelic melody. "Morning Has Broken." <http://hot.virtualpc.com/guitar/songframe.htm>

◆ [3]Allen, Charles. *A Mountain in Tibet, The Search for Mount Kailas and the Sources of the Great Rivers of India.* London: Futura Publications, 1983. p. 43.

◆ [4] Bailey, F.M. *No Passport to Tibet.* London: Rupert Hart-Davis, 1957. p. 123.

CHAPTER XI

◆ [1]Davis, Mark. *Lost in the Grand Canyon.* The American Experience, Public Broadcasting Service, 1999.

◆ [2]Kingdon Ward, F. [Sic] *Caught in the Assam-Tibet Earthquake.* NATIONAL GEOGRAPHIC, March, 1952.

◆ [3]Kierkegaard, Soren, Danish philosopher, 1813-1855. *The Quotable Climber.* New York: The Lyons Press, 1998. p. 68.

EPILOGUE

◆ [1]Ward, Captain F. Kingdon. *The Riddle of the Tsangpo Gorges.* London: Edward Arnold, 1926. p. 206.

◆ [2]Shipton, Eric. "Upon That Mountain." *Eric Shipton The Six Mountain Travel Books.* Seattle: The Mountaineers, 1985. p. 435.

ACKNOWLEDGMENTS

O MY TRAVEL COMPANIONS, Tom McEwan, Jamie McEwan, Roger Zbel, Doug Gordon, Harry Wetherbee, Doris Wetherbee. Dave Phillips, Paulo Castillo, Ang Kami Sherpa, Pemba Sherpa, Lobsang Yunden, Peme Gompa and his Lost Boys, my deepest gratitude for your partnership in the field and patient support in the preparation of this account.

To those who went before, especially Kintup, toughest and purest of us all, our boundless admiration.

To The American Canoe Association, The Explorers Club, The National Geographic Society, The Polartec Challenge Grant Program, the Henry Foundation for Botanical Research, The Excellence Foundation, Space Imaging, Mr. Adam James, The Honorable James and Mrs. Susan Treadway, and the many companies that expedited our way and made our venture possible, our sincere thanks.

And to Anita Hinders, who generously provided the line drawings that grace this text, my appreciation for your support and admiration for your skills.